GREG EGAN

Modern Masters of Science Fiction

Science fiction often anticipates the consequences of scientific discoveries. The immense strides made by science since World War II have been matched step by step by writers who gave equal attention to scientific principles, human imagination, and the craft of fiction. The respect for science fiction won by Jules Verne and H. G. Wells was further increased by Isaac Asimov, Arthur C. Clarke, Robert Heinlein, Ursula K. Le Guin, Joanna Russ, and Ray Bradbury. Modern Masters of Science Fiction is devoted to books that survey the work of individual authors who continue to inspire and advance science fiction.

A list of books in the series appears at the end of this book.

Greg Egan

Karen Burnham

UNIVERSITY OF ILLINOIS PRESS
Urbana, Chicago, and Springfield

Manufactured in the United States of America
1 2 3 4 5 C P 5 4 3 2 1
♾ This book is printed on acid-free paper.

Library of Congress Cataloging-in-Publication Data
Burnham, Karen
Greg Egan / Karen Burnham.
pages cm — (Modern masters of science fiction)
Includes bibliographical references and index.
ISBN 978-0-252-03841-9 (hardback)
ISBN 978-0-252-07993-1 (paperback)
ISBN 978-0-252-09629-7 (e-book)
1. Egan, Greg, 1961 — Criticism and interpretation.
I. Title.
PR9619.3.E35Z58 2014
823.'914—dc23 2013040329

To Charles and Gary with thanks;
To Curtis and Gavin with love.

Contents

Preface

My personal familiarity with Greg Egan's work tracks my development in both the science fiction and scientific worlds. I started reading Egan around the same time I started reading *Locus* magazine, after attending the World Science Fiction Convention in San Jose in 2002. I was just out of college with a freshly minted bachelor of science in physics and working on developing signal processing algorithms. I had been a devoted science fiction reader all my life, but discovering *Locus* magazine, with its in-depth interviews, reviews, and news of the science fiction field, made me realize that I could get much more out of my reading by writing about it. The first review I ever published in a "real" edited venue was on Egan's *Schild's Ladder* for *Strange Horizons*.

After a few years I'd learned more about the craft, and in 2007 *Locus*'s senior reviewer, Gary K. Wolfe, invited me to come to the International Conference on the Fantastic in the Arts, suggesting that I consider submitting a paper. I'd never written that sort of paper before but immediately had an idea that seemed worth pursuing. So I dipped my toe into more serious scholarly waters with a paper on the treatment of posthuman gender in Charles Stross's *Glasshouse* and Egan's *Schild's Ladder*, which later appeared in *The New York Review of Science Fiction*. Since then I've completed a master of science in electrical engineering (which gave me an even greater appreciation of stories such as "Learning to Be Me"), and I currently work at NASA's Johnson Space Center as an electromagnetic compatibility engineer.

Egan's work strikes exactly the balance between science and art that I have found valuable in my own life and career. So it is with great pleasure that I have been engaging with Greg Egan's fiction for this volume, and with immense gratitude to the University of Illinois Press and editor Bill Regier for allowing a rather unconventional science fiction scholar to take on the task. I hope that what readers find in these pages will strike an appropriate balance between consideration of literary values and some of the more scientific aspects that are also critical to understanding Egan's work.

I extend my thanks to all those who have been generous with their time as I have talked through my various thoughts on Egan's work over the past few years. Conversations with John Baez, Ted Chiang, John DeNardo, Gardner Dozois, Kathleen Ann Goonan, Daryl Gregory, James Patrick Kelly, Geoffrey Landis, Russell Letson, Karen Lord, Beth Potterveld, Paul Graham Raven, Maureen Kincaid Speller, Jonathan Strahan, and Alvaro Zinos-Amaro have all informed this volume. I need to profusely thank those who have mentored me in my engineering career over the years, especially Sud DeLand, Buzz Delinger, Michael Draznin, Mary Harris, John Norgard, and Bob Scully. I thank the late Charles N. Brown for founding *Locus* magazine and for inviting me to drive him to the airport—which favor he amply repaid with his wealth of insight, anecdote, wine, and scotch. I must especially thank Gary K. Wolfe for inspiring me to become a reviewer, for encouraging me when I did, and for thinking of me when he heard about this series at the University of Illinois Press. Without his generous feedback, and the editorial eye of Maureen Kincaid Speller, this would be a much poorer volume. All errors, of course, stem from the source, myself.

I thank my parents, Paul and Anne Burnham, for introducing me to science fiction, for letting me read whatever I wanted with no limitations, and for inculcating the habit of thoughtful conversation to which I remain addicted to this day. Many thanks go of course to Greg Egan, who has been generous with his time in conducting the interview you'll find at the end of the book, who has kept a beautifully detailed online bibliography and scientific notebook, and who has created so much fiction that is worthy of deeper thought and study. And all my thanks, forever, go to my husband Curtis Potterveld. I started drafting this book when our son Gavin was two weeks old, and before it was done we'd also moved houses. Without Curtis's vast well of patience and willingness to solo-parent, this manuscript, my sanity, or our son (probably the manuscript) would not have survived.

GREG EGAN

INTRODUCTION

Traditionally, a book-length study focusing on a single author might begin with a chapter of biographical material: parents, early childhood, family history, and the like. This book, focusing on the work of Australian science fiction author Greg Egan, will not follow the traditional format. The scant biographical details known about this multifaceted, influential author can be summed up as follows: Egan was born on August 20, 1961. His mother was a librarian. He had an early interest in film, earned a bachelor of science in mathematics from the University of Western Australia, and worked as a programmer in the medical research field. He has been writing full time since 1992. He's a vegetarian. Add in a young-adult flirtation with Catholicism and a staunch adult commitment to atheism and refugee issues, and that nearly exhausts the available biographical material.

Throughout his literary career Egan has avoided publicity and self-promotion, with occasional interviews conducted by e-mail being the exceptions. He discussed his reasons for this reticence in his first published interview, conducted in 1993 by Jonathan Strahan and Jeremy G. Byrne of *Eidolon* magazine:

> As for being entertaining in person, I'm not a public speaker. That's not my role, and it's not something I'd do well in any case. I had a job interview once where I said so little that the man who was conducting the interview—a very pompous professor of immunology—told me I was illiterate. (What he meant was inarticulate, of course, but it didn't seem wise to point that out to him.) So the day it becomes obligatory for writers to go out and cultivate fandom, like politicians on the hustings, they'd better put it in the publishing contracts so I can refuse to sign them. . . . I'd do it badly, and I also think the value of it is overrated. I've bought books by my own favourite authors for years without knowing the first thing about them, other than what they've written. It's all down to reviews, past works, and word of mouth. I believe there's a large component of the SF readership who don't even know—let alone care—about all the bullshit that goes on. Of the people I know who read science fiction, the majority have no connection whatsoever to fandom, and they're quite oblivious to whether or not Writer X has had his photo in *Locus* every month, and juggled armadillos while filk-singing at the latest Worldcon. ("Burning the Motherhood Statements")

His stance on this issue has been unwavering, as seen in this 2009 interview in *Virtual Worlds*:

> Q: You've been described as a recluse. You don't attend science fiction conventions, there are no photographs of you to be found anywhere, and very few people in the publishing industry have actually met you. Is there a reason why you value your privacy so highly?
>
> A: It's funny; I spend my long weekends mowing the lawn and visiting friends, and I get described as a "recluse" by people whose idea of normality is dashing around a dreary hotel somewhere trying to get photographed next to someone famous.

It was once jokingly noted at a World Science Fiction Convention panel that if science fiction reviewers were barred by ethics from reviewing anyone they knew personally, then the only person they could all review would be Greg Egan.

This book will also forgo any consideration of Egan as a quintessentially Australian writer. While he lives in Australia, sets some of his fiction there, and has won a number of Australian awards, his career took off in British (*Interzone*) and American (*Asimov's*) magazines, and he doesn't consider his Australianness to have had much to do with it. He dismissed the notion of core Australianness (or "Miracle Ingredient A") explicitly in his 1995 essay "A Report on the Origins and Hazardous Effects of Miracle Ingredient A" in the Australian SF magazine

Eidolon. One line serves as an example of the tone: "Yeah, and Skylab fell on us because it was homing in on Miracle Ingredient A."

Egan leaves his work to stand on its own, and that is how it will be considered in this book. At the time of this writing he has published twelve novels and sixty shorter stories. Over time we can chart a clear career trajectory that any author could be proud of: an early mix of successes and rejections, slowly finding his core themes and audience, getting published regularly, showing up in Year's Best anthologies, getting award nominations, moving from short stories to novels, and winning major awards. One can track Egan's rise to prominence in part through tables of contents: when David Hartwell and Kathryn Cramer looked at the history of hard SF in *The Ascent of Wonder* (1994), Egan did not appear, and he did not have a novel out in time to merit inclusion in the 1992 edition of John Clute and Peter Nicholls's *The Encyclopedia of Science Fiction*. By the year 2000 all that had changed. In George Mann's *The Mammoth Encyclopedia of Science Fiction* (2001), Egan's entry reads in part: "This is why many view him as one of the most successful writers of HARD SF: he does not alienate the reader with high-tech jargon but instead puts the scientific aspects of his work in understandable terms and characters with whom it is easy to identify" (130). (This has, however, become arguably less true as the new century has progressed.) When Hartwell and Cramer revisited hard SF as it appeared in the 1990s in *The Hard SF Renaissance* (2002), Egan appeared not once but twice. Farah Mendlesohn devotes several pages of the introduction to *The Cambridge Companion to Science Fiction* (2003) to a detailed reading of *Schild's Ladder*, and by 2010 Egan fit comfortably in a book titled *Fifty Key Figures in Science Fiction*, which stated: "[Egan is] widely considered one of the preeminent figures of post-cyberpunk sf" (Bould et al. 76). As we will see in chapter 1, that upward trajectory has perhaps peaked and declined in the new millennium. However, there is no doubt that Greg Egan is an important and influential author who remains a touchstone of the science fiction field.

Arguments about definitions of science fiction in general or hard science fiction in particular are perennial topics of conversation and literary analysis. However one chooses to define the terms, there is no doubt that what Egan writes is near the heart of contemporary SF and hard SF. More than any other contemporary science fiction writer, he has set himself a project of raising science's profile through art—to convince people that science is as important and critical to the human condition as romance or religion. As he puts it in the extensive interview that can be found in this volume:

> If I'm pleased with one general achievement, it's to have contributed something to the very small subset of literature that engages in a meaningful way with the full context of human existence. The fact that we are part of a physical universe whose laws can be discovered through reason and observation is the most profound and powerful insight in our history, but most literature—including a large proportion of SF—either ignores it or trivialises it. . . . A body of art that contained nothing about the laws of electromagnetism, gravity and quantum mechanics, nothing about the physical grounding of consciousness, and nothing about the *process* by which we've learnt the rules that govern everything around us, would be like a body of art depicting present day Earth that contained no mention of any human law or custom, no tension between an individual and society, and no representation of a city, a village, a forest or a river. Art that's blind to the true landscape we inhabit—physical reality in the widest sense—is just absurdly, pathetically blinkered and myopic.

I believe that this project as it relates to the intersection between art and science is laid out most clearly in "The Planck Dive," a novelette Egan wrote near the peak of his popularity. Published in 1998 in *Asimov's* magazine (edited at the time by Gardner Dozois, a major booster of Egan's fiction), the story was nominated for the Hugo Award for best novelette and won the Locus Award for best novelette for 1998. It has been translated into German, Italian, Japanese, French, Spanish, and Czech (not unusual for his fiction from the nineties). It is set in the same universe as his novel *Diaspora*, which appeared in 1997. It features software-based posthumans, the type of characters that appear in many of his most famous and successful stories, including *Permutation City*, *Schild's Ladder*, and "Glory." A detailed reading of "The Planck Dive" might be a good way to elucidate some of what makes Egan's fiction unique and important.

The story starts with an unusual image: "Gisela was contemplating the advantages of being crushed—almost certainly to death, albeit as slowly as possible—when the messenger appeared in her homescape. She noted its presence but instructed it to wait, a sleek golden courier with winged sandals stretching out a hand impatiently, frozen in mid-stride twenty delta away." This is typical of the sort of hook that Egan tends to use to invite a reader into a story. It invites the question "Why is this person considering being crushed to death?" which may motivate readers to stick with the next few paragraphs.

That's important because the next few paragraphs walk us quickly through a dense web of quantum and general relativistic physics, with sentences such as:

> Relativity demanded that a free-falling particle's rotating phase agree with every other clock that travelled the same path, and once gravitational time dilation was linked to changes in virtual particle density, every measure of time—from the half-life of a radioisotope's decay (stimulated by vacuum fluctuations) to the vibrational modes of a sliver of quartz (ultimately due to the same phase effects as those giving rise to classical paths)—could be reinterpreted as a count of interactions with virtual particles. (*Luminous* 291)

Only those readers who are really interested in the physics, or who have been sufficiently firmly hooked by Gisela and the still-frozen messenger, will make it through. That the story did so well on popularly voted awards lists (the Hugo and *Locus* Awards are both voted on by a large population of science fiction readers) indicates just how many readers have been happily willing to absorb these kinds of rigorous and abstruse physics lessons (or at least to skim them as necessary).

Egan throws out a few well-chosen names to give us a context for his projected future physics: Einstein and his theory of relativity that links space and time; Andrei Sakharov and his theorizing on gravity; Roger Penrose and his work attempting to unify quantum mechanics and general relativity (work still not complete, early in the twenty-first century); Lee Smolin and his work on quantum gravity; and Carlo Rovelli, who helped develop loop quantum gravity theory. He then mentions a physicist named Kumar, presumably in our future ("a century after Sakharov," who died in 1989), who is described as having moved the theory forward into something that could be used to make accurate predictions. This tracing of a conceptual lineage, grounding speculative physics in the work of modern physicists both well known and not, is a hallmark of Egan's stories and helps make his stories stand out even among other hard SF writers.

It becomes clear that Gisela is working on her own physics model in the run-up to a daring experiment. The eponymous Dive is an audacious proposal to manipulate the interior of a black hole to allow for computation and to send copies of several posthuman scientists into the black hole to conduct experiments. Only after grounding us in the physics relevant to the experiment does the messenger unfreeze and do we start to learn more about Gisela's environment. She lives inside a simulated reality that is physically based on a satellite orbiting a black hole named Chandrasekhar (after another twentieth-century physicist, who worked out the evolutionary sequence of stars, specifically which stars can become black holes). Egan will feature another community orbiting a black hole in *Incandescence* (2008). Gisela learns that they are receiving visitors from another VR community back near Earth—people in this future can change location by transmitting the information that defines them: "Everything meaningful about an individual citizen could be packed into less than an exabyte, and sent as a gamma-ray burst a few milliseconds long" across space (*Luminous* 292). There is no faster-than-light travel here, as Egan almost always writes fiction that plays by the rules of physics as we know them today, but this does enable light-speed travel for anyone willing to brave the trip and resulting temporal displacement (Chandrasekhar is ninety-seven light years away from Earth, meaning that a minimum of 194 years will pass between the guests' leaving home and returning to it).

The arrival of the guests precipitates the main conflict of the story. Cordelia and her father Prospero ("[Gisela] been wondering why a Prospero had named his daughter Cordelia, but now it struck her as only prudent—if you had to succumb to a Shakespearean names fad at all—not to put anyone from the same play together in one family" [*Luminous* 295]) come from a community devoted to the arts of flesh-and-blood humans from before the majority of the population uploaded into computers. This sets up a collision between "science" and "the arts" that will play out through the story.

Gisela takes Cordelia for a tour while her father's information is still being downloaded. Cordelia seems very interested and well informed about what is going on. (This gives a sense of the timescale on which the posthumans operate; for Cordelia to have been aware of the experiment at all, it must have been in the planning stage for at least two hundred years, due to the light-speed communication and travel limit.) We are treated to a visual description of what travel near a black hole would look like and how light from the stars would appear to a human observer moving closer to the event horizon. Gisela and Cordelia discuss the view, adding to our understanding through dialogue. In this case, Cordelia asks some of the questions that a reader might have, allowing Gisela to explain the physics in more detail. This dialogue-based approach to exploration of scientific ideas is a very old form—it easily goes back to Plato's accounts of Socratic dialogues, which dealt with topics of math and science as well as philosophy and aesthetics. It is also seen in Galileo's famous *Discourses and Mathematical Demonstrations Relating to Two New Sciences*, which he wrote while under house arrest. That manuscript features three speakers—Salvati explains the ideas, Segundo asks the necessary questions, and Simplicio asks the "dumb" questions that can arise through misunderstanding. Egan's work in the twenty-first century often uses this format (although almost never with a Simplicio character), especially in the novels *Incandescence, Clockwork Rocket*, and *Eternal Flame*. It becomes clear that Cordelia is firmly in the Segundo category when she points out a subtle feature that Gisela's software hasn't modeled correctly.

Prospero, on the other hand, is a caricature of an artist who not only fails to understand science, he also fails to understand why anyone would *want* to understand it. His opening line is: "I'm sure your Falling City is ingeniously designed, but that's of no interest to me. I'm here to scrutinise your motives, not your machines." He insists on shoehorning their scientific adventure into a classical mythic structure: "There's a wide range of choices besides the Pandora myth: Prometheus, Quixote, the Grail of course . . . perhaps even Orpheus. Do you hope to rescue the dead?" He doesn't fill Simplicio's role in the dialogue, simply because he has no interest in the dialogue at all. "Why am I needed? I'm here to be your Homer, your Virgil, your Dante, your Dickens! I'm here to extract the mythic essence of this glorious, tragic endeavour! I'm here to grant you a gift infinitely greater than the immortality you seek! . . . I'm here to make you legendary!" The frustration that many in the scientific community felt during the 1990s, when some sectors of academic humanities departments seemed to glorify willful ignorance about science and scientific achievement, oozes from the pores of this story.

> Sachio's owl blinked with puzzlement. "But you find the Dive itself incomprehensible. So how are you suited to explain it to others?"
>
> Prospero shook his head. "I have come to create enigmas, not explanations. I have come to shape the story of your descent into a form [poetry] that will live on long after your libraries have turned to dust."

> "Shape it how?" . . ."You mean change things?"
>
> "To extract the mythic essence, mere detail must become subservient to a deeper truth."
>
> Timon said, "I think that was a yes." (*Luminous* 308–9)

There are five members of the dive team: Gisela, Sachio, Tiet, Vikram, and Timon. The names conjure up a Star Trek–style multiracial future, but as is typical for Egan's fiction featuring posthumans, their names are just about the only thing that differentiates one from another. Gisela is clearly our POV character, but the others all seem turned from the same mold. One may be snarkier than another, or they may have different technical specialties and avatars, but the fact that one character has an implied Asian heritage and another an Indian background leaves no trace on their characterization. I believe that Egan has come a long way in terms of integrating cultural and gender differences in his characterization, but certainly this somewhat featureless approach has come to typify Egan's writing for the majority of science fiction readers familiar with his work.

After additional scientific dialogue and complaining about Prospero, the mission is launched. From the viewpoint of those remaining on the satellite, the event is over in less than two milliseconds. Then they must suffer through Prospero's rendition of "The Ballad of Cartan Null." Prospero has ignored everything Gisela and the others had told him. In his version of events, "Charon's passengers" entered "gravity's abyss" for reasons he'd invented out of thin air: to escape, respectively, a failed romance / vengeance for an unspeakable crime / ennui of longevity; to resurrect a lost flesher ancestor; to seek contact with "the gods." The universal questions the Divers had actually hoped to answer—the structure of space-time at the Planck scale, the underpinnings of quantum mechanics—don't rate a mention. Eventually, the arguments break out:

> It was Sachio who finally lost control and interjected angrily, "Cartan Null is some ghostly image of a scape, full of ghostly icons, floating through the vacuum, down into the hole?"
>
> Prospero seemed more startled than outraged by the interruption. "It is a city of light. Translucent, ethereal . . ."
>
> The owl in Sachio's skull puffed its feathers out. "No photon state would look like that. What you describe could never exist, and even if it could it would never

> be conscious." Sachio had worked for decades on the problem of giving Cartan Null the freedom to process data without disrupting the geometry around it.
>
> Prospero spread his arms in a conciliatory gesture. "An archetypal quest narrative must be kept simple. To burden it with *technicalities*—"
>
> [. . .]
>
> Sachio cut him off impatiently. . . . "What you've created is not only devoid of truth, it's devoid of aesthetic merit." (*Luminous* 317–18)

Eventually, Prospero grabs Cordelia and leaves in a huff. Gisela makes a last-minute bid to convince the girl to stay, but Cordelia decides to return with her father—both out of love for him, and hope that the two centuries that have passed since they left will have moved her home community beyond its rather insular ways. But the resolution of the character and plot arcs (Cordelia's decision to migrate or not, and Prospero's disastrous poem and the reaction to it) are not the end of the story. Now the viewpoint shifts to the participants in the Dive, where it turns out that Cordelia snuck a copy of herself on board to participate (let's not think too carefully about the implied software security, or lack thereof, that allowed that to happen): "'Freeeeee-dom!' Cordelia bounded across Cartan Null's control scape, a long platform floating in a tunnel of colour-coded Feynman diagrams, streaming through the darkness like the trails of a billion colliding and disintegrating sparks" (*Luminous* 319). We then get the rest of the story from the Divers' point of view—a couple of milliseconds to the observers back in normal space becomes hours of subjective time for the participants. As the experiment progresses, they make a major breakthrough in understanding the "why" of certain rules of quantum mechanics. Although they'll never be able to communicate their discovery to the outside world, and even though their time inside the black hole will be finite, in the end they feel that it was all worthwhile—the beauty and the elegance of what they have discovered, although not everything they had hoped for, is immensely satisfying for them.

"The Planck Dive" involves investigations into the nature of quantum mechanics and space-time under extreme conditions. These questions come up repeatedly in Egan's fiction, especially in the twenty-first century. The novel *Incandescence* tackles general relativity as experienced by a society orbiting a black hole (without the quantum mechanics), and the Orthogonal trilogy alters the equations that describe our space-time and works out large swaths of new physics and how a world based on them would operate. As is the case with many Egan stories, the two best resources for further understanding the physics that go into stories like "The Planck Dive" are *Gravitation* (the authoritative book on general relativity, by Charles Misner, Kip Thorne, and John Wheeler), and Egan's own website, which includes the equations he used to make his predictions, as well as pictures and animations illustrating the different exotic scenarios.

What we are presented with in "The Planck Dive" is a future where (unlike our own present) there is a working model of the interactions of particles in space-time: "a model of spacetime as a quantum sum of every possible network of particle world lines, with classical 'time' arising from the number of intersections along a given strand of the net" (*Luminous* 262). No experiments have disproved this model, but it is somewhat arbitrary and thus unsatisfying. In our current understanding of physics there is considerable difficulty in moving between macroscopic "classical" interactions and quantum-scale interactions, as well as understanding how the world we see arises from the non-intuitive rules governing quantum mechanics. Apparently, a lot of that confusion has been resolved in this future, but there are still questions about why the rules of the universe work the way they do.

Cordelia's tour of the black hole introduces us to the odd ways light behaves in the vicinity of a black hole. Light visibly bends in the presence of a strong gravitational field (it bends in the presence of *any* gravitational field, but we don't notice it in our day-to-day environment), and if it passes close enough to the hole, it can end up either orbiting it or spiralling into it. We learn that the space-time inside a black hole is not a homogenous flow, but a chaotic froth of light and energy and tidal forces based on the mass and light flowing in. Thus, the actual Planck Dive will consist of injecting matter and radiation into the event horizon in very specific ways in order to shape the geometry inside. This reshaping will allow light beams carrying information (the computations that will simulate the people inside) to exist for some amount of time inside the event horizon, where they will be able to conduct physics experiments at length scales much smaller than possible outside. This will enable them to test their physics model at the smallest possible distances (Planck's constant is the smallest unit of length possible in our quantized universe, hence "Planck Dive") and, with luck, learn about the physics underlying it all.

The experiment plans to make use of an extreme application of the Doppler effect. Light consists of electromagnetic waves—the light we see from the sun and the radio waves we receive on our radios are all part of the same phenomenon; they just have different wavelengths. The wavelength of an FM radio station might be three meters; the wavelength of green light is close to forty micrometers (six orders of magnitude smaller). As light gets Doppler-shifted more and more, its wavelengths will get shorter and shorter—into x-rays (a few nanometers—10^{-9}), and then gamma rays, the shortest waves on our measured electromagnetic spectrum at roughly one picometer, 10^{-12}. That is the highest-frequency (and thus most energetic) light that any known natural process can emit. However, Egan imagines that under the tidal forces inside a black hole, there would only be a theoretical limit to how short light's wavelength could become—perhaps even down to the Planck length of 10^{-35} meters. That is how the participants of the Dive hope to learn about the fundamental nature of space-time. The whole setup will act like an extra-super particle accelerator, where photons that are becoming more and more energetic (as the light achieves ever-shorter wavelengths) are colliding and producing all kinds of new particles. In much the same way that the Large Hadron Collider needs phenomenal amounts of energy to accelerate protons and smash them into each other to produce a variety of exotic particles, here the scientists are getting even more extreme acceleration and energy "for free" from the black hole's infinitely steep gravitational field.

As the experiments progress, there's the moment of breakthrough—after confirming the Kumar model at successively smaller and smaller lengths, the scientists find something that is different from the predictions. As with all the best scientific moments, there's a specific sequence of events. First, the data show something odd, so they go back and confirm the results. In this case, the data have to do with a variation on the well-known two-slit experiment in quantum physics that shows that while light is a particle (a photon) that can only go through a single slit at a time, it also has a wave structure (as in the wavelengths we have been talking about), which means that a diffraction pattern shows up (based on the phase differences of the waves) when you run the experiment over and over. Inside the black hole, the experimental diffraction pattern shows that the phase differences between these particles are quantized (not something we see in experiments we have been able to do)—but not evenly spaced. Next, all the scientists grow quiet as they try to figure out what the discrepancy *means.* This is followed by elation when one of them works out a framework allowing the new data to fit elegantly with everything known beforehand:

> Vikram shouted with joy, and did a backwards somersault. "There are world lines crossing *between the nets*! That's what creates phase!" Without another word, he began furiously sketching diagrams in the air, launching software, running simulations. . . . Gisela felt a stab of jealousy: she'd been so close, she should have been first. Then she began to examine more of the results, and the feeling evaporated. This was elegant, this was beautiful, this was right. It didn't matter who'd discovered it. (*Luminous* 325)

This is the way the process of scientific inquiry works in the real world: not quite content with the current state-of-the-art models, people devise experiments to push understanding just a little bit further. There is a moment when the unexpected happens, and then progress can be made. The exultation that comes from that moment of breakthrough is truly a rush, and I think Egan captures of the spirit of that moment as well in this story as in any of his other work.

This is especially important in this story, where he is making the strongest possible case that the narrative of science, completely separate from the narrative modes of myth, poetry, and classical drama, is just as valid and important as those more commonly exalted forms. By ending the story at the moment of scientific climax instead of personal climax, by throwing all the scientific detail into the story with no apologies, by basing the science in some of the most fundamental scientific theories known today, and by making his posthumans as human as possible while still enabling their trip into a black hole, in every way this story makes the claim that science is just as critical to human experience as art, and that it need make no apology for its "hardness." It also makes the case for "pure" science: by having the scientific climax take place inside the event horizon of a black hole, there is no possibility of technological advance based on this experiment, or even any hope of communicating it to the outside world. Even though this endeavor is completely self-contained, all the participants feel that it is worthwhile, and to the extent that we are rooting for them, so do we. This story, along with *Diaspora* (from which "Planck Dive" is an offshoot), set Egan's work on the trajectory that moved away from near-future work concerned with consciousness, identity, and bioethics toward the cutting-edge mathematical physics that underlies *Schild's Ladder*, *Incandescence*, and the Orthogonal trilogy in his twenty-first-century work.

The final line in the story (and also in the short story collection *Luminous*, where this story provides the final entry) is "That's all right. I was just curious." Curiosity is what fundamentally drives scientific inquiry, and it is something critic Russell Letson identifies as core to Egan: "I'm willing to defend the proposition that the ruling passion of Egan's work-as-a-whole is curiosity (rather a small word for what I sense in him)" and "'Curiosity' is such a watery word for what I sense in Egan. I'll bet there's some double-jointed polysyllabic German term that means 'a passion not only for structural, functional, and operational understanding but for the implications and connections that make for value or meaning.' With a side order of irony and humor, to cut the Teutonic earnestness a bit" (*Locus* Roundtable, March 5, 2012). Egan's curiosity has been wide-ranging over the years and currently focuses with laser intensity on mathematical physics. However, he has only recently turned fifty-two years old as of this writing, so there's no telling where it will take him, and us, in the next decades.

As Greg Egan is not a particularly conventional author, I have arranged the chapters of this book slightly unconventionally. Chapter 1 begins, sensibly enough, with an overview of Egan's fiction. It centers his work in the context of the "radical hard SF" promoted by the magazine *Interzone* in the mid- to late 1980s and provides an overview of his work to date, including his rise to prominence (and subsequent diminishment). I trace a loose "future history" that his stories follow, moving from biomedical advances in the near future to digital immortality in the far future. I also give a summary of some of his reception by critics to date, including the focus on his perceived lack of characterization and the various attacks and defenses that have been mounted over his work. In discussing his approach to character, I will also cover the diverse range of characters that he portrays in his fiction.

In the subsequent three chapters I tackle the three most prominent themes that I identify in Egan's fiction. These chapters are loosely chronological: chapter 2 deals with Egan's view of ethics, which can be seen from his earliest breakout story, "The Cutie" in 1989. Chapter 3 addresses questions of identity, which forms a central concern of Egan's fiction from one of his most important stories, "Learning to Be Me" in 1990, to his most talked-about SF novel, *Permutation City* (1994). Chapter 4 works through the hard-core math and physics that underpin his later novels, especially *Incandescence* (2002) and the Orthogonal trilogy (2011–13).

Chapter 2 looks at several facets of ethical concerns, including medical ethics as seen in "Blood Sisters" (1991) and "Cocoon" (1994). It also covers the uneven distribution of technological benefits, best illustrated by "Yeyuka" (1997) and the genetic engineering piracy shown in *Distress* (1995). Finally, it focuses on our ethical responsibilities to life that we create and to alien life that we may find out in the universe.

Chapter 3 covers stories that take questions of identity as their central theme. First, it looks at stories that highlight how malleable our brains are in terms of our neurochemistry. Next, it highlights stories where our consciousness is digitized, eventually becoming immortal. It uses information theory as a lens to examine some of the future consciousnesses proposed in Egan's stories and to consider what it means to divorce consciousness from physical embodiment so strictly.

Chapter 4 addresses the scientific underpinnings of several of Egan's novels. Arranged in three parts, the chapter first considers the "subjective cosmology" of the universes depicted in *Quarantine*, *Permutation City*, and *Distress*, with their attendant quantum mechanical weirdness. Next, it tackles theories about how our own universe works as seen in the novels *Diaspora*, *Schild's Ladder*, and *Incandescence*. Finally, the chapter provides a rough overview of the alternate-world physics shown in the Orthogonal trilogy, with a particular focus on *Clockwork Rocket* and *Eternal Flame*, the two volumes published at the time of writing. It concludes with a section on Egan's use of scientific principles as metaphors for larger philosophical points.

Chapter 5 concludes the discussion. I set Egan's work in the context of some broader clashes between science and society at large. Several of Egan's stories address the conflict between science and religion, and others look at the conflict between the humanities and scientific fields in academia. I apply some criticisms of pure science to various Egan stories and then end with a defense of science and science fiction as meaningful elements of human experience. After this, you will find an extensive interview with Egan in the appendix, touching on a broad array of topics, including his fiction, views on the future, and time spent working on refugee issues in Australia.

My hope is that readers will gain an understanding of Egan as more multifaceted than his reputation admits. While he is generally considered as the hard SF author who leaves all the math in, I hope to show that there is more to his work than simply equations and physics experiments.

CHAPTER 1

WRITING RADICAL HARD SF

When people discuss Greg Egan today, it is usually in the context of "hard SF." Of course, hard SF as a term is nearly as difficult to define as "science fiction" itself, but whatever it is, Egan is certainly at the center of it. In *The Hard SF Renaissance* (2002), which included two of Egan's stories, editors David Hartwell and Kathryn Cramer described him as "perhaps the most interesting hard SF writer to emerge in the 1990s" (25). Egan also served as a touchstone for several story notes in the anthology: Robert Reed "[finds himself] retreating from Greg Egan's more radical ideas" (282), Joan Slonczewski "seems closest in attitude to Greg Egan" (317), while Alastair Reynolds points him out as an exemplar in his essay "On Hard SF" (621); Karl Schroeder says, "At the moment I admire Greg Egan the most of the current generation of [hard SF] writers" (723).

What hard SF is and what it means to the field has evolved over the years. P. Schuyler Miller is credited with the invention of the term in 1957, when he used it simply to refer to the "core" of the SF field, the sort of works published, for example, by John W. Campbell in the pages of *Astounding* magazine. It was largely synonymous with what today we would refer to as "Golden Age" SF. Later, the term was pressed into service to draw a distinction between SF that dealt with physics and engineering (the "hard" sciences) and the SF being popularized during the New Wave, which often drew on the "soft sciences" such as psychology, anthropology, and sociology. Along those same lines, for a time hard SF referred to (especially in America) science fiction that had a particularly right-wing and militaristic viewpoint, such as that written by Larry Niven and Jerry Pournelle. The other options were largely confined to sci-tech problem-solving stories in the pages of *Analog* magazine (the successor to Campbell's *Astounding*).

Gregory Benford was a rare American exception to that trend. Benford, a physics professor in California, famously defined hard SF as playing "with the net of scientific fact up and strung as tight as the story allows" (Hartwell and Cramer 1994, 16)—meaning to work (write) within the constraints imposed when one obeys the known laws of physics. In its strictest formulation, none of the common SF "cheats," such as warp drive or faster-than-light communications, would be allowed. In his 1980 novel *Timescape*, Benford played with the speculative frontiers of physics, considering notions of time and the possibility of communicating backward in time using particles called tachyons (posited in 1967, they have since become a staple of television SF shows such as *Star Trek*, about as far from hard SF as it is possible to get). However, Benford sought to humanize hard SF. He lavished as much, if not more, attention on his characters and their backgrounds as he did on the physics, and he consciously adopted techniques from modernist literature in order to do so.

Also presenting an alternative to militaristic SF and problem-solving stories was the cyberpunk movement of the 1980s. William Gibson's famous novel *Neuromancer* was published in 1984, and it pushed forward the literary possibilities of examining the human/machine interface in the increasingly digital world. However, very little of the technology in *Neuromancer* and other cyberpunk stories was grounded in realistic science and technology, either from an electronics or a biological point of view. So at the same time, in 1984, David Pringle and the editors of *Interzone* magazine in Britain put out a call for what was termed "radical, hard SF" (*SF Encyclopedia*: "Interzone"). Pringle and others argued for hard SF that featured rigorous extrapolation across a broad spectrum of science; faithful both to what is physically possible and what is socially and psychologically possible, with as much attention paid to character and society as to spaceships and black holes.

Science fiction of this stripe spread from the pages of *Interzone* and flourished in the late 1980s and through the 1990s. Kim Stanley Robinson achieved widespread acclaim for his Mars trilogy, which used rigorous science and engineering to depict the near-future colonization of Mars, while his main action was driven by a dynamic and evolving sociopolitical situation seen through the eyes of a diverse cast of characters. Meanwhile, David Brin's *Earth* (1990) took speculative but not impossible physics (a microscopic black hole dropped into the core of the Earth) and used it to drive a plot that was as much an excuse for near-future social and psychological world-building on a global scale as it was a hard SF thriller.

Biology matched physics for importance as hard SF reintegrated the "softer" sciences and investigated their deeply human consequences. In 1991 Nancy Kress won her first Hugo Award (the premier award of the science fiction field) for her novella "Beggars in Spain," which uses genetic engineering to examine the consequences of inequality projected into the future. Biotechnology played a role in the fields of cybernetics and artificial intelligence that appeared in cutting-edge 1990s SF, especially that from another author who responded to David Pringle's call for radical hard SF, Paul McAuley, a British biologist. In 1996 McAuley won the Arthur C. Clarke Award (given annually for a science fiction novel published in Britain) with *Fairyland*, a tale of black-market biotech. Joan Slonczewski, a biology professor, had already brought the same level of rigor to the biological speculations of *A Door into Ocean* (1986).

It is in this context that Greg Egan began appearing regularly in *Interzone*. Very few of Egan's short stories and none of his novels broke Benford's "playing with the net up" rule. However, those of Egan's early stories which delved into neuroscience, medical ethics, psychology, and bioengineering set him solidly at the core of the radical hard SF movement and its effort to integrate hard and soft sciences.

At the same time, other early Egan stories centered on questions of digital consciousness, which lined up neatly with another burgeoning movement, the Singularity. The idea behind the Singularity is that as computer-processing power increases exponentially, artificial intelligences will quickly outstrip us, leaving ordinary humans in the dustbin of history. In 1965, Gordon Moore, the founder of Intel, formulated "Moore's law," stating that the number of transistors in an integrated circuit could double every two years. That idea of exponential increase in processing power became widely known and accepted in the 1990s. (Moore's Law continued to hold through 2012, although the rate of increase is expected to finally slow in the near future.) If you extrapolate that trend into the future and assume that intelligence / sapience is an inevitable emergent property of sufficiently complex systems, then artificial intelligence will arise and quickly outstrip the combined intelligences of all human beings alive at the time. Under one set of assumptions, the new intelligences will be to us as we are to bacteria, or at the very least they will be similarly incomprehensible. Ray Kurzweil popularized the idea in the press, and Vernor Vinge did the same in science fiction, with essays and award-winning stories such as *A Fire Upon the Deep* (1992) featuring superhuman intelligences. Charles Stross came to prominence in the late 1990s with the linked cycle of short stories known collectively as *Accelerando*, which form both an examination and critique of the Singularity future.

Egan's stories are often associated with the Singularity trope; for instance, in James Patrick Kelly and John Kessel's *Digital Rapture: A Singularity Anthology* (2012), which investigates the Singularity through science fiction stories and non-fiction essays, Egan's story "Crystal Nights" appears right alongside Vinge's story "The Cookie Monster" and nonfiction by Kurzweil. Certainly, Egan's characters have explored many facets of the posthuman experience, even if they do not follow the Singularity model point for point. However, Egan tends to reject the Singularity as a real-world concept:

> It's uncontroversial that if we could be digitized there's a lot of scope for our minds to be made faster, more efficient and less prone to various kinds of errors, but I see no compelling reason to believe in Vinge's notion of "transcendence," in which there are types of consciousness that are superior to our own in a qualitative fashion that goes completely beyond those forms of improvement.
>
> In fact, I'd say humans crossed the point about 30,000 years ago [when] we gained the capacity to reason well enough to understand any physical process whatsoever, given enough time and patience. (Burnham interview)

Even when distancing himself from parts of the field—rejecting some of the fuzzy speculations of the Singularity or cyberpunk, eschewing the social capital of the convention scene, and so on—Egan remains a key figure. For those who view hard SF as the core of science fiction, Greg Egan's work lives immediately in that core. Speculations about biology, medicine, physics, and digital consciousness, combined with a vivid imagination and a talent for evoking a sense of wonder in science fiction readers, have all contributed to cement his status as one of the masters of the field.

WORKS AND CAREER TRAJECTORY

Egan did not start out as a standard bearer for hard SF. His first novel, *An Unusual Angle*, leans toward the literary and surreal rather than the science-fictional. Of this book, published by Norstrilia Press in 1983, Egan himself says:

> For the benefit of those readers who have no idea what the book is about—most of them, I hope—*An Unusual Angle* is a kind of eccentric teenage loner story with surreal elements. The narrator literally has a movie camera inside his skull. I wrote it when I was sixteen, although I revised it slightly just before it was published, six years later.
>
> It was very big-hearted of Norstrilia Press to publish it, but it didn't do them, or me, much good. They blew their money. I laboured under the mistaken impression that I could now write publishable fiction; it took me a while to realise that that simply wasn't true. *Quarantine* is the eighth novel I've written, and the first publishable one. That *An Unusual Angle* was published at all was really just a glitch. ("Burning the Motherhood Statements")

An Unusual Angle belongs to that period of Egan's career before he became *Greg Egan*, as it were. It is a novel that is generally mainstream with a few SF and fantasy elements that make the whole thing feel somewhat experimental. It contains references to films both popular and avant-garde—presumably stemming from that time in his life when Egan aspired to be a film director rather than an author and mathematician. However, even in this early book one can see that Egan uses the language of science as a basis for metaphor: "Enthusiastic English teacher inevitably explodes with 1000 watts (RMS) of ecstasy at every record-rending result." (*Unusual Angle* 20). RMS stands for Root Mean Square and denotes a particular convention for measuring electrical power. Including it as a modifier to "watts" in a nontechnical book is excessively geeky, even for a story of high-school alienation. Evidently, the precision of science has always been an integral part of Egan's worldview.

Along with that unusual novel, Egan published eight short stories through the 1980s, an assortment of SF and horror. He was no overnight success; for him the 1980s were filled with rejection slips and novels that did not sell. But once he started getting published, it did not take long before he started getting noticed. His fifth published story, "Neighbourhood Watch" (originally published in *Aphelion* 5), appeared in *Year's Best Horror XVI* (Wagner), and his sixth story, "Scatter My Ashes," showed up in Ellen Datlow and Terri Windling's *Year's Best Fantasy, Second Annual Collection*. But the appearance of "The Cutie" in *Interzone* in 1989 really marked a turning point, establishing Egan's presence as a pure SF writer. So far, Egan has published twenty-three of his sixty short stories in the pages of *Interzone*. As he put it in the early *Eidolon* interview: "David Pringle did help steer me away from horror; when he bought 'The Cutie'—my first SF story for *Interzone*—he made it clear that he thought I was heading in the right direction" ("Burning the Motherhood Statements"). "That little nudge in the right direction," he said "saved me from wasting another ten years trying to become the next Clive Barker!" (*Aurealis* interview). In "The Cutie" a single man longs to have a child but hasn't been able to find a partner with whom to have one. He opts for a bioengineered "Cutie" of the title—a child who looks human but will never develop human intelligence and will die at around age four. He becomes "pregnant" in order to grow the Cutie—the unnaturalness of this is highlighted, which makes more sense in the context of the horror stories that precede it in Egan's publishing history—and he loves the "child" immensely. But he is devastated when the Cutie learns to speak—obviously she is developing greater-than-advertised intelligence but will still die at four. As with several of Egan's other early stories, the author's hand is obviously tipping the scales, with a narrative that at times seems manipulated instead of flowing naturally. It is difficult, for example, to believe that there would be a market for semi-human babies who die young, or that a protagonist obsessed with child-nurturing would not simply adopt. However, while this is a story that lightly hits some horror buttons, it is firmly on the side of near-future, bioethics-oriented SF.

After Pringle's editorial intervention, 1990 proved to be Egan's breakout year, with eight stories appearing in venues such as *Interzone* and *Asimov's* as well as smaller venues such as *Pulphouse* and *Eidolon*. That year Egan showed up on the *Interzone* readers' poll three times, winning with "Learning to Be Me," twice on the *Asimov's* readers' poll, and five times on *Locus* magazine's recommended reading list—an impressive showing by any measure. He continued appearing in annual Year's Best anthologies, with "Learning to Be Me" and "The Caress" both appearing in the eighth volume in Gardner Dozois's long-running *Year's Best Science Fiction* anthology series. Dozois, then editor of *Asimov's* magazine, became a major booster of Egan's work, and he has included Egan's stories in thirteen *Year's Best* anthologies to date, as well as placing them in several themed anthologies. *Asimov's* was second only to *Interzone* in its embrace of Egan's short fiction; to date, fourteen of his stories have appeared there. In his review of *Distress*, Gary K. Wolfe of *Locus* magazine noted in April 1996 that "[Egan] was the first writer to have two stories in the Dozois annual for two years running."

In Dozois's recollection:

> I first noticed Greg Egan's work in *Interzone*, where he'd published a couple of stories such as "Scatter My Ashes" that I suppose would have to be called techno-horror. When he first started sending stories to me at *Asimov's*—and, as I recall, he sent a number at once—there were both SF stories and horror stories in the batch; I encouraged him to send more SF, and indicated that I wasn't particularly interested in the horror. His early stories also tended to be short and sketchy—he'd have a great new idea in them, but wouldn't do much with it fictionally (the early stories of Charles Stross were similar); all they would really have going for them was the idea. (*Locus* Roundtable, March 4, 2012)

Looking at the stories published in that breakout year 1990, a core theme of Egan's fiction emerges with repeated inquiries into the question of identity. One of his most important stories, "Learning to Be Me," is critically concerned with identity and how it may be maintained (or not) when transforming into an immortal, digital consciousness. Even a story with only the most hand-waving of scientific premises, "The Safe-Deposit Box," wonders how a person who inhabits a different body every day could construct a coherent sense of self. In "Axiomatic" he posits bioengineered nanotech that when inhaled can literally change one's mind—rewiring neural structures in such a way, for instance, that Buddhism will seem the only possible truth of the universe or, as in the case of the protagonist, lowering one's inhibition against committing murder. What does it mean to be you when changing your brain chemistry can alter your most cherished convictions? We will continue to see Egan focusing on questions of identity through all of his short fiction and novels.

The other theme that emerged in 1990 may come as a surprise in the context of Egan's reputation as a hard math- and physics-based SF writer. Questions of bioethics are more dominant in his early short fiction than the intense speculative physics that one finds in his novels. The short story "Eugene" looks at the potential to genetically engineer a super-child and speculates about what the child's opinion of the matter might be. "The Caress" is a mystery tale that involves an eccentric rich person (a trope that shows up repeatedly in Egan's short stories as a handy way to motivate and enable sci-tech breakthroughs in SF and dramatize them) who genetically engineers and surgically alters all sorts of beings in order to recreate fantastic works of art. "The Moral Virologist" is a heavy-handed critique of those religious fundamentalists who believe that the AIDS virus is God's scourge against gays and other sinners; in this story a fundamentalist (and eccentric, independently wealthy) man bioengineers a virus to punish all those who are not monogamous—but through the intervention of the author's thumb on the scales, so to speak, he ends up condemning breast-feeding mothers to death as well. This is an obviously contrived story, and one that leaves no doubt where the author's sympathies lie. It will not be the last time that we encounter Egan's distaste for the religious mindset or for people who eschew the complexity and doubt of the scientific viewpoint in favor of the black and white certainties of some belief systems. "The Extra" (1990) is a quirky story, reminiscent of Oscar Wilde's *The Picture of Dorian Grey* (1890) and prefiguring Kazuo Ishiguro's *Never Let Me Go* (2005), again featuring an eccentrically wealthy protagonist. In this instance, Daniel Gray keeps a stable of clones to act as replacement parts for himself as he ages. This and other early Egan stories highlight possible abuses of biotech, and some have a surprising air of technophobia, although Egan's later fiction moves away from that tone.

The year 1991 brought seven more stories and similar levels of success, including appearances in Recommended Reading lists and Year's Best collections. The key story of that year may well be "Blood Sisters," which interrogates the ethics of double-blind medical trials. While it is one of the key methodological underpinnings of all of modern medicine, how can we justify giving placebo treatments that we know won't work to some patients—and keeping them in ignorance about it? Egan dramatizes the dilemma in this story about twins with a rare genetic condition, one of whom dies as a result of receiving a placebo medicine while the other, receiving the genuine treatment, survives. Another bioethics story from 1991 is "Appropriate Love," which asks how much trauma we may require loved ones to go through in order to preserve the life of a family member.

Egan's growing reputation as one of the major authors to watch in the SF field was cemented in 1992. Eight stories appeared that year, including three in *Asimov's* and three in *Interzone*. The year also marked a major milestone: the publication of *Quarantine*, his first purely SF novel and his first book published by a major press. *Quarantine* deals with the possibility that the human brain's potential to collapse the quantum wave function could be unusual or unique and addresses what the consequences of that might be. More than his other novels, *Quarantine* feels rather like cyberpunk, with a corporate-saturated future (product descriptions and prices are salted throughout the early chapters) and recurring Asian motifs (such as a New Hong Kong in Australia). When asked about the connection with cyberpunk, Egan replied:

> In fact, the way cyberpunk as a movement influenced me most was a sense of irritation with its obsession with hipness. I don't think there's much doubt that "Axiomatic" and the opening sections of *Quarantine* have a kind of cyberpunk flavour to them, but my thinking at the time would have been less "Maybe I can join the cyberpunk club!" and more "Maybe I can steal back private eyes and brain-computer interfaces for people who think mirrorshades are pretentious, and do something more interesting with them." (Burnham interview)

Quarantine is now seen as the first in a loose trilogy of books dealing with "subjective cosmology," which also includes *Permutation City* and *Distress*.

Meanwhile, Egan's short fiction for that year featured both hard and handwavy SF. "Into Darkness" posits a phenomenon where light only travels one way, so you can never see what's in front of you. It's a hard-SF puzzle-story with a thriller feel. "The Hundred Light-Year Diary" deals with the potential to send information back in time and the political control of that information.

Equally depressing in mood is "Worthless," in which a protagonist in the Holden Caulfield mold participates in a market research group and tries to use the information gathered to find his soul mate. "Unstable Orbits in the Space of Lies" echoes "Axiomatic" in that people are forced by circumstance to adopt beliefs, but here, instead of choosing beliefs and self-imposing them via brain chemistry, one is drawn to a belief system based on one's geographical location, thanks to an unexplained upheaval in space-time. "The Walk" looks again at the exact technology of "Axiomatic" and how it may take some of the sting out of dying (although it does so using a rather poorly motivated main actor). Finally, "Closer" uses the technology introduced in "Learning to Be Me" in order to walk a couple of posthumans through many permutations of trying to experience what it is *really* like to be another person.

Having published three times as many stories in three years as he had in the preceding decade, Egan's short fiction output trailed off at this point while he focused on writing novels. He published five novels in the 1990s and five more between 2000 and 2012.

The publication of *Permutation City* in 1994 confirmed the sense that Egan was one of the most important new authors of the SF field at that time. Fifteen years later, *Permutation City* comes up frequently in any discussion of Egan, especially those involving critics and other SF authors, an indication of the book's continuing influence. As Jo Walton, Hugo award–winning author of *Farthing* and *Among Others*, put it in a 2008 review: "I loved *Permutation City* when I first read it in 1994. It blew me away. It does everything science fiction ought to do—it has a story and characters and it's so full of ideas you almost can't stand up straight." *Permutation City* imagines the early days of digitizing and uploading human brains and delves deeply into the mind-bending potential for subjective experience as a digital consciousness. For instance, you can run the "code" of a person on multiple servers, or out of order, or at different speeds, and the subjective experience of being that person will remain the same. Paul Durham, one of the main characters, uses a (speculative) mathematical trick to create a pocket universe that will be infinitely self-sustaining, and he sells space in it to people who wish to ensure that their digital copies will never be erased. Multiple variations of digital experience are dramatized: One gentleman considers himself infinitely malleable and reprogrammable, rewriting himself in such a way that he can be splendidly happy churning out hundreds of thousands of lathed table legs during one period, then writing ream upon ream of comic operas for another length of time. That's one solution for the potential problem of becoming bored with eternal life—rewrite yourself to edit out boredom. Another character, a successful businessman, writes himself a personal hell as penance for a murder he committed as a young man. Other characters pour their efforts into evolving alien life in a simulated and simplified universe. The theme of evolving AIs is one that Egan would return to later, with a very different viewpoint, in the novelette "Crystal Nights" (2008).

Permutation City picks up the cyberpunk concepts of digital consciousness and computer-human interfaces, strips away the noir/thriller/gee-whiz trappings, and interrogates what it would *really mean* and what it would *really feel like*. It is no wonder that this book marked Egan's first appearance on a number of award lists. It showed up on the Locus Recommended Reading list, was nominated for the British Science Fiction Award and Philip K. Dick Award (the latter for a book receiving its first publication in paperback), and received the Campbell Memorial Award (for outstanding science fiction novel) and the Ditmar Award for Best Long Fiction (for best Australian SF—he also won the Ditmar Award for Best Short Fiction that year, with "Cocoon").

Reviewing *Permutation City* for *Locus* magazine, Russell Letson wrote:

> Egan has turned what could be a self-indulgent, anything-goes Virtual Reality fantasy situation into a dizzying and dazzling intellectual and emotional hall of mirrors, with breathtaking vistas of uncertainty, *trompe d'oeil* illusions, and recursive, self-devouring paranoid paradoxes. . . . Very few writers who have taken on this material have grappled with what it might mean to have complete control over one's subjectivity—who are you if you can be anything you want to be? Where does your identity lie? (Letson 60)

Gary K. Wolfe's review in the same magazine is more equivocal:

> What he fails to convey is any real sense of the alienness of such a state of being—his Copies cling tenaciously to useless human traits. . . . Where we expect something of the evolutionary strangeness of Cordwainer Smith or Olaf Stapledon or even Sturgeon's neoterics, we get a bunch of aging neurotics who seem to have no idea at all what to do with an almost infinitely malleable universe . . . it stops short of the kind of transcendence that seems promised by its striking premise. (Wolfe 23)

This tension between different expectations of Egan's fiction will be seen repeatedly throughout his career.

From this point, Egan's focus turned squarely to novels, although the short stories that he published continued to receive awards and recognition from critics. Egan published only two short stories in 1994, but with "Cocoon" he earned his first Hugo nomination and his first appearance on the longlist for the James Tiptree Jr. Award (for science fiction and fantasy stories illuminating gender issues). "Cocoon" is a straightforward bioethics story which asks: What if you could guarantee that no toxic chemicals could ever harm a developing fetus, but as a side effect you would also guarantee that no child would ever again be born gay? The protagonist is a contentedly gay private eye who is forced to examine the ethical and political consequences of this development.

In 1995 the novel *Distress* appeared, set at the intersection of global media, a major scientific conference, and applied philosophy. Noted short-story author Ted Chiang, who often deals with similar thematic terrain to Egan, names *Distress* as being his favorite of Egan's novels: "[It] has the most going on. . . . In *Distress* he had multiple themes that all tied together" (*Locus* Roundtable, April 21, 2012). Thanks to its portrayal of a gender spectrum that includes people who are asexual (using the genderless pronouns ve / ver / vis), this book also appeared on the Tiptree Award longlist. That same year two short stories were nominated for the Hugo Award for Best Novelette: "Luminous," about an alien threat that appears in a region of far-flung mathematics, and "TAP," which features a chip implant that changes the way humans communicate.

After a publishing gap in 1996, *Diaspora* appeared in 1997, one of the first stories in Egan's oeuvre that looks into the far future and imagines what digital consciousness independent of physical bodies could accomplish. That year also saw the publication of the short story "Reasons to Be Cheerful," which Egan noted as one of the stories that he is happiest with (the other being "Learning to Be Me"). It dramatizes and demystifies the extent to which our personalities are dictated by the neurochemistry of our brains.

In 1998 the novella "Oceanic" won the Hugo Award for its category. This story takes place in a future similar to that of *Diaspora*, but at some point the posthuman beings decided to give up on disembodiment and physically colonize an ocean-dominated planet. The main character internalizes and dramatizes the conflict between science and religion in a way that echoes Egan's autobiographical experience, set down in his essay "Born Again, Briefly" for the book *50 Voices of Disbelief: Why We Are Atheists*.

Another Tiptree-noted novel, *Teranesia* (1999), featured a gay Indonesian protagonist and dealt with "evolution, the Indian Rationalists Association, the breakup of Indonesia, quantum mechanics, and sex" (*Gigamesh* 1998; trans. Greg Egan website). Finishing off a remarkable run of stories and novels, 2002 yielded the stunningly hard SF far-future novel *Schild's Ladder*, in which immortal posthuman scientists, who can be as embodied or disembodied as they choose, argue and collaborate in response to the spread of a differently structured space-time universe that is expanding into, and wiping out, our own space-time at half the speed of light. *Schild's Ladder* was emblematic of the core of the science fiction field to such an extent that it was used as the exemplar text of modern SF in the introduction to the *Cambridge Companion to Science Fiction* (2003).

Awards voters (more of Egan's awards have come from fan-voted awards than from juried awards, the short-story-specific Sturgeon Award being a notable exception) seem to appreciate Egan's hard SF more than his near-future bioethics stories. As he moved away from medical stories to hard SF, the awards nominations and awards began to stack up—this is due both to building up a reputation over the years and to the shift in subject matter. However, voters seem to have less tolerance for this at novel length. None of his nine Hugo nominations have been for a novel.

Many readers found *Schild's Ladder* to be hard going, and it was followed by a substantial gap in Egan's publishing history while he became deeply involved in the politics of refugees detained in Australia. He spent time corresponding with and visiting the refugees who had been detained, sometimes for years, in Australia's byzantine detainment centers. Egan opened his home to those newly released and looking to start a new life.

> The detention of asylum seekers is unambiguously the worst thing that my own government is doing at present. . . . [E]very medically qualified person who's visited a detention centre describes them with phrases like "factories for producing mental illness," and in any case it's just obvious to me that locking up people for years when they've committed no crime is barbaric. But I wasn't even aware that this was happening until the government started going to extremes to politicise the issue. In 2001 they sent armed commandoes to board

> a Norwegian freighter that had rescued asylum seekers from a boat that sank en route to Australia. . . . This was a hugely politically popular move, but my response was "You've got to be kidding." I never went to Nauru, but I finally found out what was happening in Australian detention centres and that was every bit as appalling. And once I'd had some contact with the people who were actually locked up in those places it was impossible to ignore what they were going through. (Burnham interview)

In 2008 *Incandescence* marked his return to fiction. It is one of the hardest SF novels ever published, focusing on fundamental physics and reimagining general relativity from the perspective of an alien race inhabiting an asteroid orbiting a black hole. Again, many readers found it dry or too challenging.

Since then Egan has been publishing novels regularly but to little fanfare. His 2010 *Zendegi* returned to near-future SF. It is set in an Iran returned to democracy and concerns itself primarily with AI research and the near-future potential for simulating human consciousness. 2011 saw *Clockwork Rocket*, the first book in the Orthogonal trilogy, with *The Eternal Flame* appearing in 2012. That trilogy pushes hard SF as far as or even further than *Schild's Ladder* and *Incandescence*, creating a universe where the laws of physics, changed from our own by flipping just one sign in the equations of relativity, are dramatically different. To explain the world building, diagrams are included in the story and equations in the appendix, with an extensive collection of explanatory notes appearing on Egan's website. (Most of his novels have these explanatory online supplements, but those explaining Orthogonal's world building could easily constitute an entire textbook.) While in these novels he returns societal implications to center stage, particularly in dealing with the reproductive politics of an alien race, there can be no doubt that Egan has staked his reputation on the notion that pure scientific inquiry is a worthy subject for fiction in its own right, and that it is entirely fair to challenge readers to stretch their understanding of physics and math as far as it will go.

The long gap bracketed by two challenging novels marked a critical halt in Egan's forward momentum in terms of influence and popularity in the field. From 2002 to 2008 Egan published only eight short stories, and several of these appeared in venues not generally known for publishing fiction, such as *Nature* and *Technology Review*. Between the long gap and the increasingly esoteric physics underlying his stories, even near-future *Zendegi* (2010), which deals in part with politics that presciently foreshadowed the Arab Spring movement of 2011, failed to reach a larger audience.

Schild's Ladder, *Incandescence*, and the Orthogonal books have very high "entrance exams," to borrow a phrase used by Jonathan Strahan and Gary K. Wolfe in their discussions of Egan's work. By entrance exam, they mean stories that start with imposing and intimidating physics discursions that may discourage casual readers (or readers uncertain of their hard SF prowess) from reading further. Some of Egan's later short fiction also features these sorts of barriers, with "Glory" (2007) perhaps being the clearest example.

For these and other reasons, Egan's influence and success in the field has been slowly diminishing. The awards nominations have grown fewer, and while his 1990s novels were published in America by wide-distribution publishers such as EOS, all of the novels since *Schild's Ladder* have appeared from the noted small press, Night Shade Books. The one bright marker is that between "Oracle" in 2000 and "Crystal Nights" in 2008, every short story Egan wrote appeared in one or more Year's Best anthologies, a remarkable run of eight stories. Indeed, the field welcomed his return in 2007 with two Hugo nominations, for "Dark Integers" (a follow-up to "Luminous") and "Glory." Still, it appears that Egan's popularity is currently waning; in the first decade of the twenty-first century, the exciting and expanding areas of the genre have moved away from the core of hard SF where Egan's work resides. From 2000 forward, there are stronger movements in such areas as "The New Weird" (championed by Jeff VanderMeer, with an exemplar in China Mieville), "Mundane SF" (championed by Geoff Ryman) and "Slipstream" or "Interstitial" fiction (with an exemplar in Kelly Link). Nevertheless, there can be no doubt that even if Greg Egan never wrote another word, his work from the 1990s would be of lasting influence and critical importance to the science fiction field.

FUTURE HISTORY

When looking at Egan's strengths, world building is probably at the top of the list. Combining the short stories and novels, it is possible to map out a rough future-history framework in which to place Egan's technologies and themes. It should be noted that Egan explicitly rejects the notion of a fixed future history or common setting for his stories: "I'm not attracted to common settings at all. The last thing I want to do is create a future history and tie my hands by having to conform to it. All that [some of] the . . . stories you mention really have in common are some items of technology" ("Burning the Motherhood Statements"). Of course, many of his stories, including the early horror tales and those without a firm physics underpinning (for example, "Unstable Orbits in the Space of Lies"), don't fit into this structure at all, so consider this to be a general guide and an interesting exercise. For instance, fitting the stories into this framework highlights the fact that many of its stages are characterized by advancements in life extension and immortality.

We start out with near-future medical advances that extend life and health. As mentioned earlier, "The Extra" features clones kept in order to supply spare body parts to the aging rich. In "Appropriate Love" a woman carries her husband's brain in her uterus while a new body is grown for him. "Cocoon" posits medical tech to protect babies in the womb, and in "Yeyuka" the wealthy of the world have medical implants to prevent, detect, and cure common diseases and cancers.

Other near-future stories focus on technology that alters people's fundamental personality / beliefs through neurochemistry. The key story here is "Axiomatic," but the same theme also shows up in "Chaff" (gengineering for drug wars), *Quarantine* (the hero is given personality modifications by both cops and villains), and "Reasons to be Cheerful" (a brain-damaged man gets an artificial neural network implanted in order to feel pleasure again).

Next, the brain is made immortal by early implantation of an artificial neural network. This is a fascinating idea based on very real science, although the implementation would be impossible today. The neural network is "trained" for years to perfectly mimic the human brain that contains it—which is an extension of the way in which real (though very limited) neural networks are developed today. The most important story here is clearly "Learning to Be Me." The same tech appears in "Closer," "TAP," and "Border Guards" (the latter from 1999, in which a person from our era, who has known death, tries to stay isolated in a far-future society of immortals).

The stories eventually move away from the artificial neural network approach and instead toward digitizing consciousness and the creation of digital entities by scanning and uploading the brains of "real" people. *Permutation City* is the primary example of this, although the concept is also covered in "Transition Dreams" and "A Kidnapping," and its existence is implied in the background of *Diaspora*. At first, these uploads, or Copies, exist only on painfully slow servers (faster if you can afford better processors) or in robot bodies; some of these robots appear in the story "Induction," and a few remnants appear in *Diaspora*. Artificial intelligences (not based on specific humans) are created in *Permutation City*, "Crystal Nights," and *Zendegi*. In the first two stories, the intelligences are "evolved" within a simulated universe, while in *Zendegi* the AI is based on biological brain mapping and is designed for specific applications.

In time, however, these digitized people upload into robust and dedicated digital communities on ubiquitous and ample servers. This allows new "people" to be "born" without ever having been embodied—a process described in the first chapter of *Diaspora*, titled "Orphanogenesis." Another key technological development is the Qusp, or Quantum singleton processor, which allows users to take advantage of quantum computing to run their brains without taking the risk that many-world versions of themselves will be continually spawned—the story "Singleton" describes this development in detail.

Eventually these posthumans move out into space—which they can do much faster and with fewer resources than would be possible with physical bodies. When people are information, information can be sent at light speed—or run on miniature computers that can travel in tiny spaceships that go faster and with less fuel than today's spacecraft. Both these approaches are seen in *Diaspora*, "The Planck Dive," and *Schild's Ladder*.

Finally, we come to a far, far distant future in which the galaxy has reached something resembling stasis. Everyone is effectively immortal, with humans and aliens commingling peacefully in a society known as the Amalgam. In these stories, hundreds of thousands of years into the future, the real challenge is coping with the ennui of immortality. Egan being Egan, his characters tend to do this by maintaining a spirit of scientific inquiry. The key stories in this setting are "Riding the Crocodile," *Incandescence*, and "Glory."

Egan's stories also contain a significant amount of solid and sometimes prescient near-future speculation. Granted, science fiction is not necessarily in the business of realistic predictions about the future. While it is easy to point to Arthur C. Clarke and his early description of telecommunications satellites, the fact that we have not yet colonized Mars makes Ray Bradbury's stories no less haunting and effective. As Egan points out: "All SF writers make their fictional technology work by waving their hands to various degrees; even the most scrupulously logical and scientifically informed writer is making choices that let them tell the story they want to tell, rather than undertaking a sober, cautious attempt to predict the future" (*Aurealis* interview). Still, when writers depict the near future in their stories, as Egan most notably does in *Quarantine*, *Permutation City*, and *Distress*, it is interesting to see how that future looks ten to twenty years later. These three books were written from the perspective of a Western country in the 1990s. When *Distress* was published in 1995, personal computers were just becoming ubiquitous, and fewer than twenty million people worldwide had ever accessed the Internet, mostly via dial-up modems.

One important aspect of Egan's world building is restraint. Characters still travel in airplanes and stay in hotels—no suborbital transports or sleep-stasis chambers. There is little space travel until the relatively far future (roughly one thousand years) in *Diaspora*. This reflects the shift that science fiction had to make in the face of the lack of follow-up to the Moon landings, moving away from the Golden Age, wherein it seemed obvious that easy space travel was just around the corner. Instead, it is in computing and communications technology that we now see some of the most dramatic changes, both in Egan's fiction and in SF more generally. In Egan's near futures the media is relatively omnipresent: in *Distress* reporter Andrew Worth walks around with a biological implant that records everything he sees for later editing (reminiscent of *An Unusual Angle*, although put to use by a much more restrained and mature storyteller). This is presented as a very expensive program, much as only professional news stations today are likely to have high-end video cameras. But of course, our present-day cell phones and smartphones mean that very little happens outside the range of a recording device. Andrew also carries around a notepad with which he can check e-mail, make quick video edits, transfer money, and search online databases—basically an iPad. In "Our Lady of Chernobyl" (1994), set in 2013, the narrator says: "My *Schweitzerdeutsch* package came with free maps and tour guides; I hit the Where am I? button, and the GPS unit in the notepad passed its co-ordinates to the software, which proceeded to demystify my surroundings" (*Luminous* 264). The "package" may not have things called "apps," but at the time of this writing the Apple App Store has several apps titled "Where Am I?" available for ninety-nine cents each. And the voice guide in the package sounds very much like Siri, the digital personal assistant unveiled with Apple's iPhone 4S in 2011:

> "Do you wish to know more?"' the tour guide asked me.
>
> "Not unless you can tell me the word for a pathological fear of cathedrals."
>
> It hesitated, then replied with impeccable fuzzy logic, "There are cathedrals across the length and breadth of Europe. Which particular cathedrals did you have in mind?" (*Luminous* 265)

As Egan noted:

> The speed with which digital communications technology became ubiquitous certainly makes some of my stories from the early 1990s look clunky. By the time I wrote *Distress* I think I got it pretty much right—everything in the world is searchable and available wirelessly, so Violet Mosala can pull a sound bite off the web in seconds to correct a journalist at a press conference—but prior to that I was far too conservative. It's not that I didn't anticipate the potential of the technology, but I couldn't imagine that there'd be so much investment in actual infrastructure, so quickly. (Burnham interview)

Egan also has a gift for extrapolating second-order consequences. It is one thing to look at computers becoming faster and more ubiquitous and to project that trend into the future (first order). It makes perfect sense to take the nascent communication path of e-mail and project it along the same trend line. However, it takes much greater insight to look at the potential ubiquity of e-mail and see that eventually junk email (spam) will be a problem and that an arms race between spam programs and anti-spam filter programs will ensue—but that is the sort of projection we see in *Permutation City* (1992), where Maria has to look at a message that is evading her filter program's attempts to read it.

On the other hand, bioengineering has not progressed with anything near the speed of fiction. Andrew Worth has all sorts of implants that allow him to modify his own biochemistry in real-time as well as the ability to synthesize a large variety of simple pharmaceuticals. Nothing like that exists, and it does not seem to be on the horizon; nor do we have genetically engineered coral with which to build anarchist island communities.

Concerns about climate change reached a threshold of popular awareness in the 1980s and '90s, also leaving an imprint on the science fiction of the time

For instance, in *Quarantine* (published in 1992 and set in 2068) Egan mentions a worsening hole in the ozone layer leading to severe UV conditions—concerns shared by David Brin's *Earth* (published in 1990 and set in 2040). The ozone hole specifically has actually gotten better with time and strict regulation, but overall the concern with global climate change is still intensely relevant today. Egan updated his environmental concerns in *Permutation City* (1994), which lines up more accurately with the future we are living in. By *Distress* (1995) he was writing about Greenhouse refugees. These sorts of subtle world-building touches help Egan's work age gracefully. However, it is the larger themes that appear in his stories that make them influential and important many years after their original publications.

CRITICAL RECEPTION AND CHARACTERIZATION

It is not surprising that critics have had a broad range of opinions when it comes to Egan's work. As seen in Gary Wolfe and Russell Letson's paired reviews of *Permutation City*, tastes vary greatly. What seems to be universally acknowledged is that Greg Egan is a writer worth talking about. The readers of *Interzone* were some of the first to be enthusiastic about the young hard SF writer, with one letter writer commenting on "Learning to Be Me": "Greg Egan's story was particularly brilliant; I'm still considering all the implications of it. How can a short story have so much depth and so many levels?" (Mason 74). Egan topped the popularity poll of that magazine in both 1991 and 1992. In 1993 the inimitable John Clute reviewed *Permutation City* for *Interzone*: "It felt to me as though Egan was refusing to allow computers, or V. R., to 'be' anything more than he felt they could be; it felt as though—unlike any cyberpunk writer around—he totally eschewed the sweet-tooth of the generic analogue. . . . The ending is uplifting, though still acoustically perfect. Afterwards I had lightfilled fugal dreams I could not follow" (Clute 53). Similarly, Brian Stableford's review of *Quarantine* in *The New York Review of Science Fiction* said joyously: "*Quarantine* is real s.f. It is speculative fiction whose adventures of the mind are based in our contemporary understanding of what the universe is actually like. . . . By the time this fast-paced narrative enters its final phase, the author is producing new and unforeseen consequences of his line of extrapolation at 4- or 5-page intervals. Every single one of them exhibits that wonderful combination of glorious unexpectedness and seeming logical inevitability which is the main aesthetic reward of true s.f." (Stableford 7).

However, this should in no way imply that Egan's reception has involved only uncritical praise. While Egan's fiction is never less than thought provoking, those thoughts are not always positive. In discussing the collection *Luminous* and the novel *Teranesia*, Damien Broderick was ambivalent about Egan's view of humanity: "Is Egan (as artist) heartless? It can often seem that way." (*Eidolon* 28, 101), followed by "[Egan's story can be] summed up thus: we humans are rewritable gadgets with no transcendental meaning, acting in a meaningless universe—get over it" (117). During the 1999 Symposium on Posthuman Science Fiction, Egan featured prominently in the discussions. Russell Blackford noted that Rob Latham challenged Egan's "dubious premise . . . that individual personality . . . is wholly reducible to electrochemical action and may therefore be subjected to technological intervention to remodel the self." Maureen Kincaid Speller wondered how the infrastructures of the posthuman elite utopias are maintained, and Helen Merrick was likewise concerned that Egan's posthumanity ignores socioeconomic forces (Blackford 2000).

Critics and scholars have used Egan's work to discuss AI, religion, transcendence, transhumanism, gender, physics, math, identity, consciousness, the aesthetics of science and science fiction, and much else. However, a lot of the discussion of his work has centered on problems of characterization. When considering the radical hard SF of the 1990s and beyond, Egan's work fits nicely into the requirement for rigorous extrapolation in both the "hard" and "soft" science fictional dimensions. However, the fit is less comfortable when the lack of conventional characterization is considered. Egan has become *the* representative example of this issue in the wider SF field. Reviewing *Diaspora* in 1998, Gary Wolfe noted: "The weakness of *Diaspora* is also the weakness of much philosophical hard SF: it seldom deigns to spend much time wallowing in human drama, and seems impatient with itself when it does" (*Locus* 444, 16). Egan's stories are constantly characterized as cold and intellectual even by their admirers, leading to an unshakeable sense that Egan's characters are not "normal" in the way that writers in workshops are taught to regard them.

Consider Frank, the protagonist of the 1989 breakout story "The Cutie." After his girlfriend's abrupt departure he has a moment of introspection that echoes through several of Egan's protagonists: "I sat in the kitchen drinking, wondering if there was any way of persuading her to come back. I knew that I was selfish: without a constant, conscious effort, I tended to ignore what other people felt. And I never seemed to be able to sustain that effort for long enough. But I did try, didn't I? What more could she expect?" (*Axiomatic* 232–33). *Distress*'s Andrew Worth has similar problems: he has rules that he consciously develops for dealing with his girlfriend (who likewise doesn't stick around for long). And when he implicitly insults her during an argument, he notes: "Gina looked stung; I couldn't tell if she was faking" (16). There can be no doubt that these scenes resonate with readers, considering Egan's own wider characterization technique. There is a sense that when he is not paying attention, he forgets to include character details and that it takes extra effort for him to model fully human characters.

In the story "Blood Sisters" (1991) Karen is an identical twin, and thanks to medical experimental protocol, she survives a tailored viral disease while her sister dies. We never get a physical description of Karen or her twin. We get one scene from their childhood to open the story (which serves to remind the reader of the fact that identical twins share exact genetic information) and a passing mention that their parents died in a car crash when the women were already adults. We learn that Karen is a workaholic, stay-at-home hacker while her twin is a globetrotting adventurer. And Karen is enraged when she finds out that her sister was given a placebo instead of real (and effective) medication. She has a boyfriend, Martin, but barely seems to tolerate him. As she is distancing herself from his solicitousness, she notes: "Perversely, at the very same time, I missed our arguments terribly; resisting his excessive mothering had at least made me feel strong, if only in contrast to the helplessness he seemed to expect of me" (*Axiomatic* 98). This passage seems to "tell rather than show" in the parlance of writing workshops. There is no mention of how Karen and Martin met, what he looks like, or what he does. There is a sense that the characters are being modeled instead of inhabited or animated. In a mathematical or physics simulation one focuses on the critical details, leaving out complicating and extraneous factors. One suspects that for the purposes of his brand of storytelling, details such as appearance and background fall into the "extraneous and irrelevant" category. It doesn't help that Egan's initial reputation was founded on his short fiction, in which characterization may be legitimately sacrificed for concerns about length. However, even in the early novels *Quarantine* and *Permutation City*, critics and reviewers noticed this tendency.

In blog posts on *Strange Horizons* and elsewhere, there exists a phenomenon known as the Egan Defense. It can be summed up by saying that it is acceptable for characters to be flat, bland, non-existent, or indistinct because the *ideas* are the important thing. Charles Stross neatly sums up this argument: "Greg Egan's wonderful clockwork constructions out of the raw stuff of quantum mechanics, visualising entirely different types of universe, fall on the deaf ears of critics who are looking for depth of characterisation and don't realize that in his SF the structure of the universe is the character" (*SF Signal*). Obviously, a large number of readers, critics, and awards voters value what Egan's fiction has to offer, even when the characters are stand-ins for various philosophical ideas. There is also an argument to be made that in describing characters as minimally as possible, Egan is making them as universal as possible (although the fact that so many of his characters hew to the default white male standard undercuts an argument of universality). Much science fiction and fantasy literature features heroes who are somehow special or better than their fellow humans. Egan's characters tend not to fit that mold. On a fundamental level, they are no smarter or better than anyone else. In order for them to win the day, they have to *understand* the universe as opposed to simply *manipulating* it. Egan makes it clear that no natural phenomenon is beyond our ken. Any of us has the core capability (whether or not we choose to use it) to understand everything about the universe.

Matt Denault has a neat rebuttal to this line of argument: "If Egan is trying to convincingly argue that the capability for understanding the universe is inherent in human life, then it seems to me crucial that he provide convincingly human characters who reach this understanding. Otherwise Egan's arguments are suspect" (*Strange Horizons* "Reading Egan").

To continue the debate, Egan has responded directly to interview questions about his approach to characterization:

> There's a preconception in some circles that the characters in realistic fiction ought to have a certain quota of relationship problems, family issues and emotional baggage of various kinds—and some people seem literally unable to believe that a real human being can be more passionate about scientific ideas than anything

> else, even though the history of science is littered with people for whom that was true. I write about characters for whom the events of whatever story I'm telling are among the most important things in their lives, and there's not much point writing about science through the eyes of someone who'd rather be down the pub. ("Interview: Virtual Worlds")

It is important to remember that there is no single monolithic "Egan character." Over twenty years and sixty short pieces, his stories have ranged from the gloriously abstract to the intensely personal, and his characters vary from the most distanced scientist to the emotionally immersed journalist. This can vary even within a single book. Gwyneth Jones contrasted the "Wang's Carpet" short story / chapter with the rest of *Diaspora*: "Egan brings his concept of posthuman polises to life . . . like digitally rarefied Italian Renaissance republics. For the rest of the book the questions are academic, the answers are worked examples, textbook style, and the characters are hardly more than present-day infotainment presenters dressed up in software-entity suits" (Jones 101).

All science fiction seeks to humanize the problems and potentials of scientific and technological advances. Simply by choosing fiction as his vehicle, Egan ventures into realms of emotion, character, and society that a mathematical thought-experiment would lack, and he fits comfortably in the SF of the '90s that sought to humanize hard SF. However, it is telling that so many people accept the criticisms of flat characterization as true—that is to say, despite whatever evidence one can point to on the other side, it seems to be more true than not. The extent to which that represents a failing of Egan's writing depends on how much a reader appreciates Egan's strengths and is willing to overlook the weaknesses.

SCIENTISTS AS CHARACTERS

Egan's fiction gives us a glimpse into the mindset of those people for whom science is their most passionate way to engage with the universe. His characters may be male or female, gay or straight, Indonesian or Persian, embodied or software—but they are (almost) always scientists. This attribute so overwhelmingly dominates their character that they tend toward a certain sameness. In addition, that mindset is rare enough that it strikes many readers as somewhat implausible that anyone "thinks that way," much less that it would be the case for an entire diverse cast of characters. Perhaps Paul Graham Raven said it best when he pointed out: "Mountain climbers are recognisably human, but the vast majority of humans are not recognisably mountain climbers" (*Locus* Roundtable, March 4, 2012). And when one looks at online communities today such as sci.physics (to which Egan occasionally contributes), it is easy to imagine that an Indian scientist and a British scientist may have more in common with each other than with a random selection of their fellow nationals.

In many of his stories, the characters function as scientists more than anything else. In *Diaspora*, the characters spend a lot of time considering multidimensional spaces, both in terms of mathematical topology and the structure of the universe. In *Schild's Ladder*, the universe is endangered by a scientific experiment that (despite following a rigorous and thorough system of peer review and evaluation) created a new and expanding form of space-time. The characters at the forefront of the action are scientists studying the border of the new region, seeking to understand it better and eventually either to reach an accommodation with it or collapse it back to nothing. In *Incandescence* an entire population slowly mobilizes to become part of a scientific effort to understand their world and its environment in order to prevent their eventual destruction. This is also true of the main characters in the Orthogonal universe.

For these characters, being "a scientist" goes far beyond an official job title, although many Egan characters are professional scientists as understood today, such as the inventor in "Singleton" or the researcher in "Mitochondrial Eve." However, the "scientist" attribute also describes the thug in "Mister Volition," the hitman in "The Walk," and the free-floating consciousness in "The Safe Deposit Box." Even the private eye of *Quarantine* has a surprisingly scientific worldview. And just about every far-future human entity we encounter in *Diaspora*, *Schild's Ladder*, *Incandescence*, "Glory," and "Riding the Crocodile" turns to the joys of scientific discovery to stave off the ennui of immortality. These characters question fundamental aspects of the universe, taking a subject and examining it in the most rigorous way.

The narrator of "Learning to Be Me" is not officially a scientist, but he spends a goodly portion of his adult life investigating neural network technology and its implications. These characters also work out hypotheses and test them. This avenue is not available to all of them, but the mugger in "Mister Volition" is being entirely (if entirely unethically) scientific when he goes to kill someone just to try to observe the "I" that might make that decision. He has a hypothesis (that some core ego, the prime decision maker of the brain, would reveal itself given a clear-cut and critical decision to make), a method of taking measurements (the Recursive Visions eyepatch and Pendemonium software), and a clear definition of what success or failure would look like. At its very core, this is the scientific method: testable hypotheses applied to repeatable phenomena. One of the most important things that Zak and Roi do in *Incandescence* is to test the system of weights in the Splinter—and when it doesn't agree with the ancient map they have, they seek to understand and explain the discrepancy instead of assuming that the old knowledge must be true.

There is a class element to the "scientist" archetype that cannot be ignored: in order to partake in these intellectual pleasures, access to education is necessary. It need not be a world-class education—many enthusiasts, including Egan himself to an extent, are self-taught in their specialty—but there is a requirement for educational resources (libraries, online info, and the like) and leisure time to pursue these endeavors—or even better, tenured university positions. Perhaps the most utopian aspect of Egan's digital futures is the idea that everyone will have this sort of leisure time. This way of spending an immortal life may strike some as unrealistic, but we can see in the background of these stories that many of the immortals turn to the arts to while away their time instead—they are just not the characters Egan chooses to focus on. Much as obsessively dedicated scientists are somewhat rare in our society, they may be a bit eccentric in the Amalgam future as well. There are those, and one may speculate that Egan is among them, who would find no better pastime for their future immortality than being able to conduct astrophysics experiments over extremely long timescales or to work out new mathematical theorems. While that is not most people's idea of a fun eternity, those who do think that way needn't be dismissed out of hand.

CHARACTER DIVERSITY

When looking at human characters in the more near-future time frame, Egan's stories feature a degree of diversity that is indicative of the gradual movement in the SF field in the 1990s and beyond toward greater inclusivity.

While an Egan protagonist is often a white male Australian named Martin (Martin being the name of the protagonist in *Zendegi*, "Oceanic," and "Yeyuka," among other instances, as well as the hero's partner in "Cocoon" and "Blood Sisters"), early on Egan also featured protagonists or major secondary characters from the Asian and Indonesian countries closest to Australia. His fiction features gay and gender-queer protagonists with some regularity. Given the concerns about Egan's approach to characterization, the diverse descriptions of these characters might sometimes appear to be largely window dressing. However, his stories have arguably been progressing in terms of their depth of characterization, with novels such as *Zendegi* and the Orthogonal trilogy examining in greater depth the specific concerns that characters who do not fit the white, straight, male default experience.

Over time, Egan's characterization has developed somewhat independently along axes of race, gender, and sexuality. Through the 1990s he was considerably more innovative on the axes of sexuality and gender-queering, hence his occasional appearance on the Tiptree Award recommended reading list. Gay relationships featured prominently in Egan's second decade of writing. Prabir's relationship with Felix is the most grounded part of his life in *Teranesia* (1999), James has a long-term relationship with Martin in the Hugo-nominated "Cocoon" (1994), and Robert Stoney (a fictionalized Alan Turing) is comfortable with his homosexuality in "Oracle" (2000) (also Hugo-nominated), even when his 1950s contemporaries are not.

Egan also began queering gender fairly early in his career. As he put it in a 1998 interview: "In general, I don't think SF has begun to explore the possibilities for trashing gender stereotypes—and ultimately trashing gender itself. A lot of what passes for 'SF about gender' just implies that we're sentenced to repeat the worst mistakes of the past over and over, for the next ten million years" (*noise!* interview, 1998). The couple in "Closer" (1992) defaults to a male/female pairing, but in their quest to use digital brain transfers to truly understand each other, they swap genders in every possible combination. Perhaps Egan's most radical reimagination of gender occurs in *Distress* (1995). This near-future world presents a broad and socially accepted gender spectrum. It goes from ufem (ultra-feminine) to en-fem (natural female) to ifem (intermediate feminine) to asexual to imale to en-male to umale. Asexual persons use the ver/ve/vis form of gender-neutral pronouns. People can modify themselves away from "natural" genders in both directions: either to become near-caricatures of masculinity and femininity (umale and ufem) or to hide their gender identity altogether (asex). The ifem/imales are described as "not at all 'halfway toward' androgynous; it was far more distinctive than that. . . . [T]he first ifems and imales had modeled the human visual system and found completely new clusters of parameters which would set them apart at a glance—without rendering them all homogenous" (*Distress* 135). Of course, almost no two people do this in the same way: "The only thing that one asex person necessarily had in common with another was the view that vis gender parameters (neural, endocrine, chromosomal, and genital) were the business of no one but verself, usually (but not always) vis lovers, probably vis doctor, and sometimes a few close friends" (*Distress* 45).

The rationale that hero Andrew Worth mentions for these gender migrations is "the most common reason people cite for gender migration: that they're sick of self-appointed gender-political figureheads and pretentious Mystical Renaissance gurus claiming to represent them. And sick of being libeled for real and imagined gender crimes. If all men are violent, selfish, dominating, hierarchical . . . what can you do except slit your wrists, or migrate from male to imale, or asex?" (*Distress* 47). That seems like a rather unlikely set of abstract and political reasons for tinkering with gender identity—a subject that is intensely personal and subjective. This can be seen as part of a pattern where some of Egan's characters are more likely to be motivated to act on behalf of abstract Big Ideas (for example, belief systems in "The Walk," pure math in "Glory," quantum unity in "Singleton," and so on) instead of smaller, quirky, personal concerns.

In an interview, Egan commented: "SF ought to be the ideal place to invent new possibilities for human interaction, but there's a lot of conservatism even in SF. In *Distress*, the main character falls in love with an asexual person, someone who's chosen to have no gender at all. One reviewer in an SF magazine fell over laughing at the very idea of this. He literally couldn't conceive of two people being in love without some form of genital friction" (*noise!* interview). By the time that digital persons form the majority of humanity in *Diaspora*, most people choose to leave gender behind them and use the vis/ver/ve pronouns. Being identified as "he" or "she" is unusual in that story. Moving further into the future, characters in *Schild's Ladder* and the Amalgam stories ("Riding the Crocodile," *Incandescence*, and "Glory") use traditional gender pronouns, which Egan explains:

> In *Distress* (and even in *Diaspora*) there were people with conventional genders as well as those without, so I used the genderless pronouns to distinguish the two cases. In *Schild's Ladder* ancestral gender dimorphism has completely vanished, but I wanted to avoid making a big deal of that, so I thought it was better to use a translation into present-day English that sounded as natural to the reader as possible. In *Distress* when there's an asex character, that's strange and significant to the protagonist, so it's OK to do something with the language that jars and brings attention to itself. On reflection I'm not sure that it was the right decision to keep using those pronouns in *Diaspora*, and to be honest I'd grown a bit sick of them by the end of that book! (Burnham interview)

The assumption is that in a posthuman future we will largely leave traditional sex, sexuality, and gender behind. However, in the relationships portrayed in Egan's futures, it is assumed that more-or-less monogamous pairings will continue to be the norm. In "Oceanic," *Incandescence,* and "Riding the Crocodile," monogamous couples are front and center. (*Schild's Ladder* and *Diaspora* don't foreground romantic pairings, but those that are featured are also generally monogamous.)

Throughout *Schild's Ladder*, Egan uses "anachronauts" to critique and satirize the social expectations of science fiction. The anachronauts are astronauts from our future (far enough in the future to use cryogenic suspension for slower-than-light space travel, but not so far as to have quantum computer digital backups). They aim for a likely star system and suspend themselves during travel, then defrost themselves, land, and talk to the people they find there. "When they left Earth, they knew they'd be overtaken by newer technologies; they knew they'd be traveling into the future. . . . They wanted to witness what humanity would become" (*Schild's Ladder* 133). Tchicaya tells the story of one group that makes landfall six times in fourteen thousand years. They are obsessed with the sex wars, with how women and men struggle for power throughout the centuries. "Nobody could bring themselves to break the news that the sole surviving remnant of human sexual dimorphism" was gendered pronouns for different personal names, the same way some languages have different gendered forms for various inanimate objects.

The various planets where landings occur invent different stories of exotic and barbaric sexual mores, and the anachronauts eat it up. On Crane they tell a story that sounds a lot like Joanna Russ's "When It Changed" (all men wiped out by a plague, the struggles to adapt, with monosexuality winning out). "On Makela, the people insisted that their planet had been peaceful since settlement. The anachronauts were terribly suspicious, and kept digging for the awful secret that no one dared reveal" (*Schild's Ladder* 135). After hearing about the anachronauts from the other planets, they make up a story about a Sacred Pentad family arrangement that is reminiscent of Ursula K. Le Guin's *sedoretu* quad relationships depicted in "Unchosen Love" and "Mountain Ways." "But the anachronauts were thrilled by the great 'cultural richness' they had finally uncovered. Apparently, their definition of 'cultural richness' was the widespread enforcement of any social or sexual mores even more bizarre and arbitrary than the ones they'd left behind" (*Schild's Ladder* 135). In a complete rejection of the entire concept of intersectionality, one couple tells the anachronauts The Truth: "And apart from trivial local details, like the exact age of sexual maturity and the latency period between attraction and potency, he and his lover embodied a universal condition: they were both, simply, people. There were no other categories left to which they could belong" (137). (The anachronauts, of course, decide not to believe them.)

This reflects the liberal hope for the future that has existed for decades, in which issues of race, class, sexuality, and gender all cease to matter and people will simply be accepted as individuals. While that idea continues to be a powerful goal to strive for, before it is reached it has led to erasures of some people's identities and lived experiences. This is an area where Egan's fiction has changed considerably since his blossoming around 1990. His early approach to characterization often glossed over or ignored less "relevant" details such as appearance (including race) and background. In *Quarantine*, Nick Stavrianos is described as having jet-black skin, but that is simply due to a common skin treatment that helps combat UV exposure; it has no social or economic ramifications. His last name is Greek, but we learn little about his background and almost nothing about his childhood. In *Distress*, Violet Mosala is an African woman and mother based in Cape Town, South Africa.

While this leads to some additional questioning of her by silly anti-science groups, it seems to have had no effect on her work, academic career, or travels. While she is not the main character in *Distress*, she is the subject of Andrew Worth's documentary project, and nothing of the struggles faced (today) by women in the sciences and academia comes across in his interviews with her. In *Teranesia*, Prabir Suresh is a product of his specific childhood—he loses his scientist parents as the result of an action by warring factions in the Indonesian islands. However, once he and his sister manage to find a home in Canada with their aunt, there is little sense of their being part of an immigrant community in Canada.

Compare this with the more recent *Zendegi* and the Orthogonal trilogy. In *Zendegi*, the story takes place mostly in Persia, and Egan traveled to Iran specifically to learn more about the geography and the feel of the place. He posted an Iran Trip Diary on his blog. When asked why he chose to set that story in that place, he responded: "I'd just spent five years in the company of people from the Middle East and south Asia, to the point where it would have felt peculiar and unnatural *not* to write something about that region. I wasn't interested in writing a depressing story about the plight of refugees—I'd already got the impulse to do that out of my system with 'Lost Continent'—and the most plausible location for a story with a real science-fictional component was Iran, which is a technologically advanced country with a highly educated population" (Burnham interview).

Martin is a Westerner who marries a Persian woman and then worries how his son will be raised after his wife dies and he (Martin) is diagnosed with terminal cancer. His relationship with his son and his Persian friends and relatives is the core of the book. The other point-of-view character is Nasim, a computer scientist. We meet her as a postdoctoral student at MIT, taking the day off to stay glued to the news about a revolution in Iran. Her family fled Iran as part of an earlier political action, and when the situation stabilizes there she moves back. As part of the software company she works for, she worries about staying on the good side of the religious authorities, as well as competition coming from India. Her ethnic and national identities are much more important to her character and narrative arc than were Violet Mosala's.

Incandescence returns to very simple characterization. It features an alien civilization alongside the Amalgam posthuman future; the society of those aliens is simple and tangential to the plot. Everyone has work to do, and as the threat from the black hole looms larger, the alien society becomes more creative and flexible to deal with it. The aliens mobilize a massive scientific and engineering effort; the story doesn't depict any artistic society worth mentioning. *Incandescence* stands as Egan's most purely thought-experimental book, with almost everything stripped away aside from the threads of scientific discovery. In contrast, the alien society of the Orthogonal universe stands on its own and is more thoroughly developed. While in many ways it is reminiscent of our own, with a default capitalist structure and typical university politics, there is a thread that deals entirely with gender and reproductive politics.

The aliens of the Orthogonal universe possess a malleable body type, able to extrude new limbs at will. Children almost always come in pairs, one male and one female. When a woman matures, she eventually splits into quarters to become four new children, which the male then raises. They say that something is "as impossible as knowing your mother," since the mother is literally erased when she has children. This can happen either as a matter of choice, or, if put off too long, it can happen spontaneously. Contraceptive drugs can reduce the chance of a spontaneous splitting, but they are highly politicized, and at the beginning of the novel they are banned. When the heroine Yalda moves to the city to study at the university there, she falls in with a group of women professionals forming the underground base of something like a women's rights movement. One of their most important tasks is securing and distributing the contraceptive drug. Yalda is not exactly a typical female in her society: as well as pursuing a high degree of learning, she lacks a male sibling. She is twice the size of a normal member of her species; when her mother started to split there was an error in the process and Yalda maintained all the body mass while developing a single new personality. This makes her stand out and occasionally causes problems based on stigma and prejudice, but it also makes her less likely to be forced to end her life through childbearing.

> When I started planning Orthogonal, my main concern was simply to ensure that the biology of the aliens wasn't too similar to our own. But as soon as the idea of reproduction by division occurred to me, it was clear that it could work on all kinds of dramatic, emotional and philosophical levels. All mothers die giving birth: how could that *not* be a source of enormous internal and external conflict?

> [. . .]
>
> As for the gender politics, if women are generally going to divide while they're still young enough for their co to raise the children, then in terms of political power they're starting out with a massive disadvantage. Apart from everything else, they'll literally be a minority, because of their much shorter life expectancy. I think it's almost inevitable that under these conditions most societies would start out with huge disparities in educational opportunity and reproductive choice. (Burnham interview)

This is the first time that Egan's fiction has foregrounded the different social pressures placed on men and women, particularly in the sciences. It is not particularly controversial to note that in the process and culture of modern Western science, being a woman and a mother implies quite different challenges than being a man and a father. Very little science fiction has recognized the sense of women and mothers in the sciences being passed over, ignored, *erased* as bluntly as Egan does here. There is also traditional sexism: when Yalda goes to a senior (male) scientist to ask for an allocation of research time on the university's telescope, here is the elder's response:

> "I've never had much time for you, Yalda," he said. "Not because you hail from the benighted eastern provinces, with your quaint dialect and bizarre customs; that can be endearing, and even correctible. And not because you're a woman—or almost a woman, or something that might have been a woman if nature had taken its proper course."
>
> Yalda looked up, startled. She hadn't been insulted in quite such an infantile fashion since she'd left the village school. (*Clockwork Rocket* 51)

In *The Eternal Flame*, the second volume of the trilogy, the tensions over reproduction become heightened. The story has moved onto a generation spaceship, and the population on that ship is critically constrained with regard to resources. The story opens with one man's co splitting into four children, as is normal, and two of the children having to be euthanized—no population growth can be allowed. Most women are starving themselves to help prevent spontaneous splitting and hoping that eventual splittings will yield only two children instead of four. They are also taking as much of the (scarce) contraceptive as can be produced. Along with the fundamental physical research being done by the physics teams (necessary to return to their homeworld), there are biologists working on better ways to control reproduction. As the biological research progresses, they hit upon a way to induce a woman to give birth to a single daughter and survive the experience herself—a radical shift that would affect everything about their society and biology. Egan says: "Philosophically, this seemed like a perfect opportunity to explore the naturalistic fallacy: the idea that whatever nature has produced is the way things should be. In our own society this is sometimes bound up with religion, but I don't think that's the only way it arises. So although these aliens have no religion, many of them do take the attitude that nature provides a kind of ideal template for life, and their role is to accommodate to that, not to fight it" (Burnham interview). A faction of the crew reacts violently to these proposed methods, and they attempt to wipe out the research and the researchers. Even the more moderate characters are disturbed by what this implies for the future.

Egan's recent fiction has taken a more thorough and nuanced approach to exploring the interactions between science and culture. Instead of projecting simplified or idealized societies to serve as a backdrop to purely scientific stories, he has invested time in placing characters in context and working out what the consequences are for individuals who vary from the cultural default in various ways. This sort of attention was lacking in his early stories and novels, and his efforts in this direction bode well for his future work.

CHAPTER 2

ETHICAL STANDARDS

Ethics have long been an important concern for science fiction as it looks to the future: how can we move out into the universe without perpetrating the worst abuses of the past? Greg Egan has considered ethical issues from his very earliest publications. He tends to hold his characters to the highest ethical standards within the framework of his stories. His near-future biotech stories consider the ethics of medical research and clinical practice from a number of different angles. When he writes about genetic engineering and AIs, he invites us to consider our responsibilities to those sentient entities we create ourselves. And when he writes about contact with alien civilizations, he asks us to consider on what basis we approach other intelligent beings, no matter what their level of technological development. Over the course of more than two decades of storytelling, Egan's fiction has set a high bar for ethical conduct toward all life, intelligent or not, DNA-based or not, with plenty of scorn heaped on those who fail to clear that bar.

MEDICAL ETHICS

Although his university degree is in mathematics, Egan has experience with the medical sciences from his time as a computer programmer:

> I spent six months unemployed—this was in 1983, at the tail end of the last recession—writing several bad novels, then finally got a job as a computer programmer with a medical research institute attached to a Sydney hospital. I stayed there for four-and-a-half years. All my formal education was in the physical sciences, so I was lucky to get a chance to hang around doctors and biochemists, picking things up by osmosis. ("Burning the Motherhood Statements")

And he feels that it is important to link things to our biological reality every now and again:

> Biology, and neuroscience in particular, turns the abstract, philosophical fact that humans are matter like everything else into a tangible set of insights and possibilities. Just knowing that we're some kind of collection of molecules only gets you so far; we're a very specific kind of thing, so if you're interested in what it means to be matter, the biological sciences are enormously important. If you want to know where love, morality, kindness, jealousy, fear and joy actually come from, the answers are all biological. (Burnham interview)

One of the stories that most clearly dramatizes the consequences of relaxing medical ethics is "Blood Sisters." Identical twin sisters have a rare genetic condition and are infected with a newly developed version of a genetically engineered virus that targets the condition. They both receive the experimental treatment, but one of them lives and one of them dies. The surviving sister realizes that, according to established medical protocol, her sister was almost certainly given a placebo as part of a double-blind trial—except that they were not told that a placebo would be one of the options. In the wake of these genetically engineered viruses being unleashed, one of the legislative measures implemented during the (indefinite) crisis was removing the necessity of informed consent in medical trials. It is proposed that keeping the patients in the dark produces better-quality data at the cost of lying to patients about the risks they face. The surviving sister starts a political campaign to push for legislation that would reinstate informed consent in medical treatment, and she begins a hacking campaign to ensure that the automatic pharmaceutical machines always dole out real medicines instead of placebos. She rationalizes this by arguing that if doctors have been lying to patients, it is just as ethical for her hacked data systems to lie to the doctors about patients' receiving placebos.

This story encourages us to question not just the three-minutes-into-the-future scenario of emergency medical protocols but the human consequences of even double-blind trials. As one journalist in the story puts it: "A good medical researcher has to care more about the quality of the data than about any one person's life. . . . And the more accurately a drug can be assessed, well, perhaps in the long run, the more lives can be saved" (*Axiomatic* 104). Egan is not the first to mine this territory; Sinclair Lewis addressed the human cost of research protocols as early as 1925, in *Arrowsmith*. However, in a very short story that packs an effective intellectual and emotional punch, "Blood Sisters" puts a particularly interesting spin on the "good of the few versus the good of the many" question by focusing more on the issue of consent itself than on outcomes. It feels counterintuitive for an author so closely associated with the hardest of hard SF to question the standard protocols for conducting scientific research. However, the idea of duplicity and misrepresentation is always represented as a fundamental betrayal of science and ethics in Egan's fiction. If both sisters had been told of the protocols, they would have known what they were signing up for. In this sense there is a significant difference between research into fundamental physics and mathematics and medical research. There is no obligation to inform electrons when we are studying them, and no need to apologize to a uranium atom for splitting it.

Several other stories illustrate negative consequences of bioengineering, but these have easier targets. In "The Caress" an eccentric billionaire pays for exotic creatures to be genetically engineered in order to replicate fantastic paintings in real life. In the story, he seeks to reproduce "The Caress" (1896) by Fernand Khnopff, a Belgian symbolist painter. The painting shows a young man, perhaps Greek or Roman, in the adoring embrace of a chimera—a creature with the head of a woman and the body of a leopard. The villain of Egan's story kidnaps people, performs plastic surgery on them, has a suitable chimera created, and contrives scenarios such that the different actors in the paintings will have the appropriate emotional relationships. In "The Moral

Virologist" a fundamentalist Christian genetic engineer (probably not the most common intersection of personal beliefs and profession) takes part of his father's fortune from TV evangelizing and engineers a virus that should kill anyone who takes multiple sexual partners. He believes he is visiting God's wrath on sinners. Unfortunately, after he releases it he realizes that it will also kill breastfeeding mothers and their babies—not a wrathful god's usual targets. This is a direct satire on that vocal religious segment in the 1980s and early '90s that claimed that AIDS was God's way of punishing gays (ignoring the hemophiliacs and other people needing blood transfusions). In "The Extra" a Dorian Gray–style eccentric billionaire keeps clones of himself for spare parts (a precursor to both Michael Marshall Smith's *Spares* and Kazuo Ishiguro's *Never Let Me Go*). When he eventually has a brain transplant performed to transfer himself into a fully new and perfect body, part of his brain is left in a decrepit and mute body, still conscious of its treatment as leftover meat. Generally speaking, people who use their wealth to impose their will on others don't come off well in Egan's stories.

The other short story that most clearly deals with issues of bioethics is "Cocoon" (1994), which was the first of Egan's stories to be nominated for a Hugo Award. The "what if"' core of this story can be neatly summarized: what if there were a way to protect a growing human fetus from most kinds of environmental harm: pollutants, alcohol, viruses, and so on. Nothing would pass the placental barrier except necessary nutrients and oxygen. The catch is that as a side effect, such a mechanism would also guarantee that no one would ever again be born gay (by blocking some of the mother's hormones from affecting the fetus). Would that be a worthwhile trade-off? This premise is based on a view of biological determinism of sexuality that has not yet been proved by research, but "Cocoon" develops its different arguments and illustrates the politicized nature of all such questions very effectively.

Although Egan has portrayed gay or bisexual characters (or people for whom sexuality is simply irrelevant) many times, this story foregrounds the sexuality of the narrator. James is an investigator looking into the bombing of a medical research-and-development facility. He is also a gay man. His partner is gearing up for a gay-pride parade, which James thinks is a bunch of pointless posturing, now that gays have legally equal rights and widespread cultural acceptance (the story is set in the mid-twenty-first century). However, as he learns about the fetal-barrier technology, it becomes evident that these are still hot-button issues, no matter how enlightened the age. Both sides (pro- and anti-barrier tech) look to manipulate media coverage on the issue. It turns out that regardless of any "accidental" side effect the barrier may have, the research company has been quietly moving gay employees away from the project. James has to decide whether to stay on the case, realizing that he's been backed into a corner where his actions will be interpreted in light of his sexuality instead of standing on their own. If he takes down the pro-gay activists, it will be a gay man that does it, demonstrating that the investigation is unbiased. If he drops the case because he is gay, it will suggest that gay people are biased. In the end, James realizes that although it may not matter in an abstract way that a hundred years hence there may be no gay people left (he repeatedly uses the metaphor: what if no one was ever born left-handed ever again?), "the only path which could lead there would be one of lies, and wounding, and vilification" (*Luminous* 155). The story is very aware that these kinds of decisions cannot be made without engaging with some very messy, often irrational, politics.

Egan's fiction paints a rather cynical view of the healthcare industry as a whole and the insurance industry in particular. For example, as the narrator of "Appropriate Love" is being told that she will have to carry her husband's brain in her womb for two years while his new body is being grown, she thinks:

> I nearly said, angrily: You won't *insist* that I do *anything*. I didn't, though; I didn't have the energy to make a scene—and it would have been a hollow boast. In theory, the decision was mine alone. In practice, Global Assurance were paying the bills. They couldn't dictate treatment, directly—but if I couldn't raise the money to bridge the gap, I knew I had no choice but to go along with whatever arrangements they were willing to fund. (*Axiomatic* 269)

In medical scenarios more than in other realms, Egan seems sensitive to the power imbalances, the "consent" that is extracted under considerable stress and through no small measure of duress. In *Distress*, the spokesman for the Voluntary Autists points out:

> Medical technology is about to go supernova. In case you hadn't noticed. So what's all that power going to be used for? The maintenance—or creation—of

> "health." But what's health? Forget the obvious shit that everyone agrees on. Once every last virus and parasite and oncogene has been blasted out of existence, what's the ultimate goal of "healing"? All of us playing our preordained parts in some Edenite "natural order" [. . .] Whoever claims the authority to define the boundary between *health* and *disease* claims . . . everything. (*Distress* 69)

This belief in and policing of a "natural order" is an issue that will drive part of the plot in *Clockwork Rocket* and *Eternal Flame*, where large segments of society resist reproductive advancements that interfere with the "natural order" of things. Looking at those stories in Egan's work that touch on the medical industry, the digital disembodied future becomes all the more tempting: no doctors or politicians defining "normal" and insisting that the populace conform; instead people would be able to "heal" or "harm" themselves as they see fit, with few (if any) implications for the wider society. It would be a future of quite literal "self-actualization."

UNEVEN BENEFITS OF TECHNOLOGY

William Gibson famously said: "The future is already here—it's just not very evenly distributed" (Gibson 1999). That applies as much to bioengineering as to anything to do with computers or the Singularity. For one thing, there's a reason why so many of Egan's short stories are driven by eccentric rich people—the rich will almost always benefit first from cutting-edge research. One of Egan's few stories that really focuses on the disparities between the First and Third Worlds is "Yeyuka," which first appeared in *Meijin* 56 in 1997 and was then reprinted in both the Hartwell/Cramer and Dozois-edited Year's Best anthologies for that year. In this near-future story (set roughly in 2020 or so), most cancers and contagious diseases have been eliminated in developed nations, thanks to a technology called HealthGuard. As Martin, the first-person narrator and a doctor, explains:

> I touched the ring on my left index finger, and felt a reassuring pulse through the metal. Blood flowed constantly around the hollow core of the device, diverted from a vein in my finger. The ring's inner surface was covered with billions of tiny sensors. . . . So the ring knew exactly what was in my blood. It also knew what belonged, and what didn't. Under its relentless scrutiny, the biochemical signature of a viral or bacterial infection, or even a microscopic tumour far downstream,

> could never escape detection for long—and once a diagnosis was made, treatment was almost instantaneous. . . . The ring could manufacture a wide range of drugs from raw materials circulating in the blood . . . . (*Infinity Plus* website)

People can wear these devices continuously, as Martin does, or they can visit a shared unit weekly or access one during a visit to a general practitioner. It is an expensive technology, but in the West it is largely ubiquitous. "The day I'd installed it, my life expectancy had risen by fifteen years—and no doubt my bank's risk-assessment software had assumed a similar extension to my working life, since I'd be paying off the loan I'd needed to buy the thing well into my sixties."

At the beginning of the story, Martin's foremost concern is losing his job. Thanks to HealthGuard, the need for cancer surgeons has dropped precipitously. Martin volunteers to spend three months working at a clinic in Uganda, a country where even the shared units are a scarce commodity. In Africa the health workers are seeing a new contagious disease, called Yeyuka, that the HealthGuard technology has not yet been able to cure, at least not officially. It turns out that the HealthGuard company has collected plenty of data on Yeyuka; the disease helped them perfect their cancer screening technology. However, since Yeyuka only affects poor people in Africa as yet, HealthGuard never bothered to spend the time and money to program a cure into the machines. The African doctors have done so, using pirated data from HealthGuard and a series of cobbled-together parallel processors, but if they ever upload that program onto a certified machine, it would be recognized as bootlegged and the machine would be turned off. They need Martin's help to get a black-market machine that they can operate themselves.

This isn't a terribly deep dilemma—it is wrong to be able to cure a disease and then to decline to do so for monetary reasons. There is no question in the story that we are meant to side with the boots-on-the-ground beleaguered clinicians. However, given the entanglement of the free market with healthcare provision the world over, we are also reminded that this sort of decision is currently made every day. We don't have the resources to cure everyone in the world of even those classes of diseases that are curable right now. This story rather ham-handedly accepts the stereotype of suffering Africa but nonetheless also asks very pointed questions about the structure of the global healthcare industry.

GENETIC PIRACY, ANARCHY

Distress is another narrative that shows significant sympathy for biotech piracy. In this near future, biotech is the most important driving technology; no mention is made of brain-uploading. Bioengineered algae produce hydrocarbons that have made oil drilling obsolete (a rather optimistic hope). The key setting for the novel is the island nation of Stateless, which is entirely the product of pirated bioengineered organisms. Stateless's political situation is very tense, as some island chains such as Fiji have been playing by the rules, growing new islands and paying biotech companies for the privilege. Their reward is billions of dollars of debt that won't be discharged for a century or more. The residents of Stateless are, however, effectively members of an anarcho-syndicalist collective. Most nations boycott the nascent country, but Stateless accepts refugees from all over, resulting in a vibrant and diverse community.

The two sides of the argument are neatly summed up in the interior musings of journalist-protagonist Andrew Worth:

> In theory, a patent lasted only seventeen years—but biotech companies had perfected the strategy of reapplying for the same coverage from a different angle when the expiration date loomed: first for the DNA sequence of a gene, and all its applications . . . then for the corresponding amino acid sequence . . . then for the *shape* and *functionality* (irrespective of precise chemical makeup) of the fully assembled protein. I couldn't bring myself to simply shrug off the theft of knowledge as a victimless crime—I'd always been swayed by the argument that no one would waste money on R&D if engineered lifeforms couldn't be patented—but there was something insane about the fact that the most powerful tools against famine, the most powerful tools against environmental damage, the most powerful tools against *poverty* . . . were all priced beyond the reach of everyone who needed them most. (*Distress* 116)

While there is no easy answer, the above paragraph hints at the narrator's sympathies. These concerns happen to presage some of Paolo Bacigalupi's recent work, starting with "The Calorie Man" in 2005 and continuing through *The Windup Girl* in 2009. In these stories Bacigalupi describes the exhaustion of the world's oil supply combining with the corporate ownership of all food crops (through patented genetic modifications) to produce a world of disruption and scarcity. In the absence of oil, he imagines that muscle power (either that of genetically engineered animals or of humans) could be harnessed for industry instead. Of course, muscle power is ultimately derived from food, and all food is controlled by corporations. In "The Calorie Man" specifically, Bacigalupi ruminates on the idea that simply growing a tomato could be an illegal act of rebellion. In his stories, the tensions result in grim dystopian scenarios.

In *Distress*, Andrew has a chat with one of Stateless's long-time residents, grilling him about the anarchist lifestyle, which is neither a dystopia nor a utopia. The street artist he talks to is comfortable walking away from his easel, but not because he has faith no one will steal it—rather, he has an alarm tag that will let him know if anyone does. Nor is the society communistic, as it allows for private property and a cash economy. There are groups that form what might as well be local governments, and principles exist that might as well be laws. The basic understanding is that the people who have emigrated to Stateless generally want freedom and stability, and they are acting in ways to ensure that their society stays stable and free.

Stateless is supposed to differ from all the other places where people like to be stable and free and yet are burdened with lots of laws and rulers, violence and chaos. For one, Stateless began in 2025 and has no history, no immediate baggage. Everyone is starting on a roughly equal footing, as emigrants with enough resources to emigrate there. As Andrew's reluctant guide puts it: "People turn up here with a slightly higher than average level of idealism. They *want* Stateless to work, or they wouldn't have come. . . . [T]hey're willing to be more flexible and tolerant than the average person who chooses to live elsewhere . . . because that's the whole point" (*Distress* 152). It is not a state that was born from violence or other forms of revolution.

The artist admits that things have started off ideally, but that may not last. He pins his hopes for the future on the fact that all the children on Stateless are educated about sociobiology:

> If people understand the biological forces acting on themselves and everyone around them, then at least they have a chance of adopting intelligent strategies for getting what they want with a minimum of conflict . . . instead of blundering around with nothing but romantic myths and wishful thinking, courtesy of some dead political philosopher. (*Distress* 153–54)

Transparency and information access are critical for this imagined society. People arrange themselves in groups called syndicates, and by convention the finances of these organizations are public. This allows people to sanction syndicates that may not be contributing their fair share—all on an informal basis, of course.

Andrew thinks of this as "Informed Anarchy" and finds it very attractive, although he still has doubts that it can survive without being twisted into its own rigid ideology. While this seems somewhat naive, it illustrates an optimistic faith in the power of education and rational thought. This puts a burden on the populace to seek out available information on politics and political structures and to act on it, an effort for which people may lack the time or patience. Over and over again in Egan's fiction we see the rewards available to those who put the effort into deep thought and engagement on any number of topics, from politics to philosophy to physics. However, that level of effort and personal responsibility may not strike everyone as particularly practical, especially people on the poorer end of the economic spectrum who have to work extra time or multiple jobs to make ends meet. To suppose that such patterns of thought can bring about the end of some of the worst chaotic cycles of human history is optimistic in the extreme.

MONEY AND POLITICS IN RESEARCH SCIENCE

"Mitochondrial Eve" (1995) directly addresses the conflict between science and religion. Specifically, the story takes a stand against religious appropriation of scientific results. The story was written after the popularization of the idea of a "Mitochondrial Eve" in the late 1980s (*Newsweek* did a cover story on the concept in 1988). Unlike nuclear DNA, mitochondrial DNA is passed directly from mother to child—it is not mixed with the father's DNA. The idea behind Mitochondrial Eve is that there is one individual who lived in Africa roughly two hundred thousand years ago whom all humans today can claim as a common ancestor.

The story begins in 2007, when a cult has arisen around the concept of this Eve, the thrust of which is to emphasize the commonality of all peoples: their slogan is "One World, One Family." Paul is a postdoctoral student in physics, and his girlfriend Lena invites him to a Children of Eve center to be mitotyped. Though the group's highly polished and culturally targeted PR techniques, used to promote their belief around the world, instantly puts Paul on edge (and Leni Riefenstahl is mentioned), this initially seems to be as harmless a cult as can be imagined. As Lena puts it: "This Eve belongs to everyone, equally. Every culture, every religion, every philosophy. Anyone can claim her as their own; it doesn't diminish her at all" (*Luminous* 30).

At first, the cult of the Children of Eve seems to represent a benign use of scientific understanding for enlightenment and positive social ends. When Paul's research funding for investigations into examining molecules for signs of a quantum entanglement history runs out, his girlfriend encourages him to get a research grant from the Children of Eve. The investors have no idea what his research means (they reference such plausible-sounding, made-up New Age titles as *Schroedinger's Lotus* and *Heisenberg's Mandala*) but have lots of money to throw around, and they appreciate the PR victory Paul could potentially produce. The idea is that his research would take the guesswork out of such variables as mutation rates and branching points. While Paul is occupied, the propaganda war starts in earnest as another group of researchers claims to have found a twenty-thousand-year-old common *male* ancestor for Northern Europeans. The Eve cultists go down to protest the Adam adherents, effectively admitting that the science is less important than the ideology. It does not take long before violence breaks out, first at a paleogenetics conference, then spreading to larger venues. Multiple "Adams" are identified by different groups, and people start pushing for genetic purity—the exact opposite of the original goal. Paul finally releases research that proves that none of the Adams—or Eves—was ever actually real, that there is no "recent" common ancestor to whom everyone can trace their own ancestry. "The truth was just too gloriously messy and complicated to serve any political purpose at all" (*Luminous* 56). Stories such as this argue against the ideological appropriation of scientific results, with the implication that only close adherence to the scientific method and objectivity can keep science pure, as it were. Certainly, it is a cautionary tale that warns against allowing research to be hijacked.

Problems with research funding and its ethical implications also appear in *Teranesia*. Prabir's parents were research scientists on an island in Indonesia when they were killed by an attack from one side in a civil war. Afterward, Prabir and his younger sister make their way to Canada as refugees. Prabir does his best to respect his parents' memory and raise his sister as they would want. He tries to keep her safe, but she returns to Indonesia as part of a biology research team. As he tags along with another researcher, he realizes that "his parents had published nothing in all their years on the island. They'd taken money from Silk Rainbow. They must have made a similar deal [to not release research data until a corporate sponsor can make use of it]. . . . It shouldn't have stung so much. They'd made one small compromise in order to do something that otherwise would not have been done at all. *When had he started thinking of them as flawless?*" (*Teranesia* 192).

In much the same way that he is in favor of openness and consent in medicine, Egan's stories come down strongly on the side of transparency and data-sharing in the sciences. When more teams can play with a given set of data, useful and productive avenues of research can be explored in parallel. *Teranesia* offers an example of this when Prabir manipulates one of the scientists into releasing her data. A team in São Paulo uses it to make rapid progress toward identifying new genes common to several new species. In *Distress*, there are three different scientific teams converging on a Theory of Everything, with the arguments between them sparking further creativity. In his far-future visions Egan creates a world where there is never any need to keep scientific data secret, where any number of teams can take any number of approaches, and people can contribute or not to the pursuit as it pleases them. Even in *Schild's Ladder*, where disagreements over what to do about the nova space eventually lead to violence, the opposing teams share data and resources to learn everything they can about the impinging space-time region. *Diaspora* is the best example of a culture of scientific openness and sharing, as many teams and individuals participate in research endeavors in both the solar system and the wider galaxy. In these futures, there is no question of begging for resources or being beholden to those who pay the bills.

ETHICS IN RELATION TO CREATED LIFE

If stories such as "Blood Sisters" deal with the ethical relationships that may guide "normal" people, stories in which the same questions are applied to created beings, whether biological or digital, are even thornier. "The Cutie" (1989) is perhaps the earliest of Egan's stories to tackle the question. In that story a man desperate to have a child buys a bioengineered creature that looks and acts like a human infant but without the mental capacity for development that a normal baby would have. It also has an artificially short lifespan of roughly four years. As the story progresses, it turns out that there's been an error—his Cutie begins to develop language skills, calling him "Daddy." He is shocked and horrified that this little being, closer to human than he thought, will be condemned to an early death. But he is self-aware enough to ask at the end of the story, "Had she never said a word, would I really have fooled myself into believing that her death would have been less tragic?" (*Axiomatic* 244). The story leads us to ask ourselves, "Why would it have been all right, so long as the child was mentally stunted, but not now that she was developing language?" On the other hand, all children are mortal—so is her death any more or less tragic than that of any other "real" child?

"Eugene" (1990) provides another perspective on bioengineering children. Bill and Angela are hapless lottery winners who want to have a child. Since they have been having trouble conceiving naturally, they go to a high-end fertility clinic. When the celebrity doctor realizes just how much money they have to burn, he uses them to fund just about every scheme that he can think of for prefertilization and in-utero child improvement. The first line of the story promises them the world: "'I guarantee it. *I can make your child a genius*'" (*Axiomatic* 37). Even before the child is conceived, it is named Eugene (for "eugenics"—when Egan is at his most satirical he is also at his least subtle).

The punch line of the story comes when the as-yet-unborn—in fact, the as-yet-unconceived—Eugene contacts his yet-to-be-parents (based on a rather hand-waving explanation involving the clinic's computer simulation of the potential embryo). Eugene has decided that the way to Nirvana is to "never have been," and he tells his "parents" that he is going to take steps to prevent his own existence.

> Angela was distraught. "But . . . why would you waste your talents on destroying yourself, when you could have lived a happy, productive life, and done great things for the whole human race?"
>
> "*Why?*" Eugene frowned. "Don't ask *me* to account for my actions; you're the ones who would have made me what I would have been. If you want my subjective opinion: personally, I can't see any point in existence when I can achieve so much without it—but I wouldn't call that an 'explanation'; it's merely a rationalisation of processes best described at a neural level." He shrugged apologetically.

> "The question really has no meaning. *Why* anything? The laws of physics, and the boundary conditions of space-time. What more can I say?" (*Axiomatic* 53–54)

There is no doubt that the celebrity scientist heading the clinic is a caricature of any number of near-charlatans today and that his arguments in favor of rigidly controlling every aspect of a child for maximum success (everything from height to taste in music) are not meant to be taken seriously.

"A Kidnapping" (1995, original to the *Axiomatic* collection) does not deal with children but moves instead to artificial intelligences. A man receives a call from an anonymous criminal group claiming they have his wife as hostage and will begin torturing her if they do not receive a ransom. He immediately calls his wife, and it turns out she is fine. What the criminals have is a perfect digital *copy* of his wife—the sort of perfect copy that could fool even her husband. The presumption is that this is a similar level of scanning technology as seen in *Permutation City*—the technology is not yet ubiquitous and Copies run on slower-than-real-time servers but are generally accepted to have the same level of consciousness as "real" people. When she finds out about the "hostage" and the ransom demand, his wife feels absolutely no connection to the copy at all—as an artist, she slices up one of her self-portraits and points out "in mock amazement, 'That didn't hurt a bit'" (*Axiomatic* 172). However, her husband cannot bear the thought of something so much like her—something probably conscious enough to believe itself to *be* her—being harmed and put through pain and torture. Without his wife's knowledge he agrees to pay a ransom in perpetuity as long as the software copy is deactivated, never run again, and never harmed.

Interestingly, his wife has never had a scan or Copy made—but the husband did. The kidnappers have broken into his Copy and based their version of his wife on his memories of her, not on the woman herself. They know that while he would not pay ransom for the 100 percent accurate version of himself, he would always end up paying to keep the twice-removed-from-reality Copy of his wife from harm. In another layer of the story, it turns out that the husband has plans for digital immortality, but this scenario has no attraction for his wife. The arrangement he makes with the kidnappers is that when he dies and his Copy is fully instantiated, they will release their copy of his wife to live with him. He knows that this is against his "real" wife's wishes, but he does not want to face digital immortality without her—or at least something he can pretend is her.

The disregard people have for their own Copies feels entirely realistic. When there are two versions of "you," one with control and one without, the one with the control will always feel like the "real" one, with perhaps as little emotional attachment to a Copy as to a photograph of yourself. However, establishing the difference between a version of someone else in physical space versus digital space is much trickier. Since, as in "Closer," we can never truly know what it is like to be someone else, we must always rely on the models of other people who live in our heads. We don't truly "know" them, but on some level we know our models of them. And we are used to dealing with people at a distance: through letters, e-mails, or phone calls. So it would be easy to feel as strongly about a friend's Copy as you do about the real person. As for your own Copies, consider Thomas Riemann's treatment of his in *Permutation City*—consigning it to an eternal, surrealistic Hell as penance for the crime of passion that the "real" Riemann committed in his youth. Does the penance count if the "real" Riemann does not experience it? That is an existential question left open in the narrative.

There is also a throwaway line in *Distress* that has interesting implications. Some AIs may be programmed to learn like children instead of being programmed to emerge as fully functional from day one. "**Kaspar** was the next generation of pseudo-intelligent software. . . . [It] was going through a learning phase, more anthropomorphically styled than anything previously attempted. Personally, I found it a little disquieting . . . and I wasn't sure that I wanted a clonelet—a pared-down copy of the original—sitting in my notepad, enslaved to some menial task, if the full software had spent a year singing nursery rhymes and playing with blocks" (*Distress* 221). Egan goes down this road again for the AI child in "Singleton" (2002); Walter Jon Williams has addressed it in "Daddy's World" (1999), and Ted Chiang has done a thorough treatment of the same premise in his 2010 Hugo Award-winning novella, "The Lifecycle of Software Objects."

"Crystal Nights" (2008) uses a classic SF trope that goes back to Mary Shelley's *Frankenstein*: the man who creates life. Egan's story closely parallels Theodore Sturgeon's 1941 novelette, "Microcosmic God." In both, a man creates a new species of life using evolutionary techniques: killing off those specimens not performing to specifications and allowing "better" individuals to breed. In Sturgeon's story the scientist maintains complete control of his biological creations and eventually harnesses their problem-solving abilities to save himself from a military assault by outsiders. This is a rather chilling "happy" ending, given how ruthlessly and horribly he tortures and abuses his creations. However, "Crystal Nights" returns to the Frankenstein model of dealing with this sort of creator/creation relationship. Daniel Cliff is a billionaire industrialist who wants to bootstrap AI life to invent new and improved computer equipment for him to market. He hires computer programmers to create a virtual landscape with enough challenges for AI life to have to evolve to overcome them. He is given ample opportunity to think through all the pain and suffering he is going to inflict on these beings; the opening scene has a brilliant AI researcher turning down his job offer because she does not believe anyone has the right to inflict that kind of pain and suffering on sentient beings, no matter what palliative measures are brought to bear.

As the AIs grow and evolve, they eventually reach a state where their "physical" form is adequate; it is their culture and thought processes that need to evolve. To "minimize" suffering, Daniel calls a halt to killing off inadequate specimens, making them effectively immortal. However, he does not have infinite computing resources, so he also calls a halt to births, making them all effectively sterile. After that point, much of the creatures' cultural and scientific development is aimed at figuring out why they have lost their children and how to regain their fertility.

When they have developed far enough, Daniel chooses one individual to talk to, and he introduces himself. He explains everything—how their evolution was directed, and toward what end. In response, far from helping Daniel achieve his aims, the AI creatures manage to port themselves and their original computer substrate into a pocket universe, the creation of which causes a massive explosion that almost kills Daniel and effectively demolishes his research lab.

"Crystal Nights" represents a changing viewpoint toward AI creations in Egan's fiction. As he offers in the Dust Theory FAQ on his website related to *Permutation City*:

Q6: What do you regret most about *Permutation City*?

A6: [. . .] What I regret most is my uncritical treatment of the idea of allowing intelligent life to evolve in the Autoverse. Sure, this is a common science-fictional idea, but when I thought about it properly (some years after the book was published), I realised that anyone who actually did this would have to be utterly morally bankrupt. To get from micro-organisms to intelligent life this way would involve an immense amount of suffering, with billions of sentient creatures living, struggling and dying along the way. Yes, this happened to our own ancestors, but that doesn't give us the right to inflict the same kind of suffering on anyone else. (*Permutation City* FAQ)

In "Oracle," hero Robert Stoney says: "A computer, programmed to pursue arithmetic as Professor Hamilton has described, is subject to far more deprivation than that child. If I'd been raised with my hands and feet tied, my head in a sack, and someone shouting orders at me, I doubt that I'd have much grasp of reality—and I'd still be better prepared for the task than such a computer. It's a great mercy that a machine treated that way wouldn't be able to think: if it could, the shackles we'd placed upon it would be criminally oppressive."

This can also be seen at the end of *Zendegi*. In that novel, technology with the ability to scan a real person has not yet been perfected. Videogame companies are competing to see who can come up with a technique to make nonplayer characters (NPCs)—the background characters the players might encounter in an adventure game, such as shopkeepers, knights, soccer players, and so on—as realistic as possible. Several techniques are advanced toward this end, some of which are based on composites of large numbers of people. Others are based on scans of specific celebrities: a Persian company works with a champion soccer player to offer gamers the chance to compete against him virtually. The protagonist of the novel, Martin, is dying and will leave behind a young son. He works with a relative at the game company to make a composite version of himself, one his son will be able to talk to after he's gone.

He runs the composite through all sorts of tests, and as he gets closer to the end of his life he pushes the copy as hard as he can. Eventually, the copy breaks down, losing its temper in a way Martin is sure he never would. He realizes that there is no way that this copy can act as a proxy for him as his son grows up, and he regrets the mental trauma he inflicted on it. The novel concludes: "*If you want to make it human, make it whole*" (*Zendegi* 278).

Again, in "The Lifecycle of Software Objects," Ted Chiang points out that if, after creating objects with that level of consciousness and putting them through all that directed learning, we treat them as nothing more than convenient and helpful slaves (which is their role in most SF; think of the wise-cracking ship's AI in so many SF stories and movies), that is an ethical lapse of stunning proportions. Both Chiang and Egan agree and make clear in their fiction that at the point where we create anything resembling lifelike AIs, we will need to ensure that we give them rights and see that they are treated well, lest we end up repeating some of the injustices of the past.

FIRST CONTACT SITUATIONS

One aspect of the trope of artificial life concerns the interesting thought experiment of first-contact situations with creatures of our own making. This trope has been part of science fiction since its earliest days, when Dr. Frankenstein takes one look at his creation and promptly takes to his bed in a prolonged and agonizing swoon. One has the impression that he really had not thought things through. In contrast, characters in Egan's fiction spend a lot of time thinking and talking about first-contact scenarios, and they play out in different ways. The earliest iteration occurs when the inhabitants of Permutation City decide how to approach the newly evolved and sentient inhabitants of the Autoverse. One of Paul Durham's main goals with the Autoverse is to create a situation where the inhabitants of that universe will *know* that it is created. In our own universe we live in doubt, hence the endless religious/scientific arguments as to whether the universe requires a creator or if it *just happened*. Durham asks Maria to create a "Garden of Eden" scenario. This is one in which the observable first state of the Autoverse universe (computationally speaking) could not be the result of any prior state. That is, things have to have had an identifiable artificial starting point, they could not have evolved from some other "natural" configuration. In theory, when Durham contacts the Lambertians (as the Autoverse residents are known) and claims to be their creator, that will be a truth empirically verifiable by the aliens themselves, instead of their needing to rely on faith as humans do when receiving visions of a god or gods.

While in some ways mirroring the development of life in "Crystal Nights"—physical evolution reaches an adequate level after which cultural and scientific progress becomes more important—the human proprietors of the Autoverse have not interfered with or directed the Lambertians' development the way Daniel Cliff did. After observing the Lambertians for millennia, the Permutation City residents, known as Elysians, decide that the Lambertians have advanced sufficiently in their understanding of their own universe to understand the Elysians' role in things. Originally, the community had decided not to contact the Lambertians until the Lambertians had constructed their own computers and simulated their universe to some degree, but these aliens have developed a means of conducting scientific inquiry through communal dance—imagine it evolving from the dances bees use to direct each other to flower beds—and have no need of computers.

Competing proposals for first contact suggest sending in an expedition immediately to explain the origins of their universe or waiting until the Lambertians come up with a hypothesis for their universe that includes the Elysians (or some other creator being) and then meeting with them as equals. The latter, more conservative approach wins popular support with little controversy—and the team waiting to make first contact is happy, given that they are sure those conditions will be met relatively soon.

There is a subtle point where the characters ask: Why not model the Lambertians and see how they will react to first contact? After all, that is where the excitement and unpredictability comes in; it is the question everyone wants answered. The reply is that simulating a conscious entity without its informed consent is deeply unethical; any simulation with adequate fidelity would be a conscious entity in its own right. When you consider that software Copies of "real" people are having this conversation in a virtual world about simulating the beings that are the result of a simulation, the discussion becomes almost vertiginous.

The complication and resolution comes about because of the physics of the pocket universe that the Elysians have created for themselves. Paul Durham discovers that while the Autoverse simulation can be slowed down, it can no longer be stopped or frozen. The Lambertians' existence is on some level undermining the rules of the pocket universe of the Elysians. At the point where the Lambertians figure out a model of their universe that does not include Creators—the Garden of Eden scenario notwithstanding—the Elysians' universe is pushed aside in favor of the Lambertians' reality. This causes a mass exodus of the Elysians into a new pocket universe, abandoning the original to the Lambertians. In both *Permutation City* and "Crystal Nights" the creators lose control of their creations (which comes as no surprise), and the creations make a break for their own space and reality. This is not necessarily presented as a question of morality: while Daniel is clearly a Frankenstein figure, rightly laid low by the creations he treated poorly, the Elysians acted with all due attention to their ethical responsibilities yet simply lacked the foresight to predict what would happen when the two simulated universes came into conflict.

Of course, first contact is very different when the interaction is with something created specifically so that the creators can talk to it someday. In treating the more traditional scenario of first contact with an independent alien race, *Schild's Ladder* provides an interesting pair of contrasting scenarios. The first is told in flashback. Tchicaya, the main protagonist, grew up on a planet where the inhabitants take community very seriously. When one member leaves to travel to a nearby planet, all the other inhabitants slow down their subjective time rate, so that for them the same amount of time will have passed as for their compatriot traveling on a relativistic journey. (Remember that if one twin stays on Earth and the other takes a near-light-speed journey out and back, the twin on Earth will be much older than the traveling twin, according to general relativity.) Tchicaya and his childhood friend Mariama break out of the slowdown for a bit of adolescent fun, the equivalent of breaking curfew. While out and about in a world of glacial adults, they discover a small patch of alien life growing on the cooling vanes of an under-utilized power plant. In this future, at this time, only four planets have ever been found to have any alien life at all, and none of the life was at a point where humans could communicate with it. In each case the entire planet was abandoned so that the indigenous life could continue its progress without interference, a relatively easy sacrifice to make for immortal beings with a galaxy's worth of planets to live on. However, Tchicaya does not want to uproot his entire planet's community. If they make such a sacrifice of time simply to avoid being out of step with one member, how much more disruptive would it be to clear off the entire planet and move to a new one? He and Mariama make a pact to keep silent about their discovery. Presumably, when everyone returned to real-time and the power plant resumed full capacity, the alien colony was destroyed. The burden of that decision devastates Tchicaya and Mariama's relationship.

Fast forward a few thousand years, and they find themselves in a similar situation but on a much larger scale. The main plot of *Schild's Ladder* concerns an expanding region of alien space-time. It is incompatible with our own space-time and is converting ours to theirs (not out of intent but simply through the rules of mathematics and physics) in a spherical region with a boundary expanding at half the speed of light. No one knows what is inside that sphere; all they can do is study the boundary. Tchicaya is in favor of studying the sphere as much as possible and trying to reach an accommodation with it, even though its expansion has meant that several inhabited planets have already had to be abandoned (although with no unintentional loss of life). Mariama is on the side of those who want to stop its expansion and shrink it back down, restoring our universe to its normal state.

At the end of the novel, Tchicaya and Mariama have the opportunity to broach the border and explore what is on the other side. They find that the new space-time universe can support an abundantly diverse ecosystem of life. There are more kinds of life in a single nanometer of that space than on an entire planet in our universe. They go exploring, eventually get in touch with some intelligent beings, and begin to hammer out a solution to their problems. Here, there is very little waffling: once they find intelligent life to talk to, there is no hesitation about opening a dialogue since the stakes are both high and constrained by time. Readers do not discover the results of their efforts, but there is no doubt that the right path is to try to find a mutual accommodation.

In the Amalgam future of "Glory" and "Riding the Crocodile," there are many kinds of alien life, and the only challenge is making sure that communication protocols are adequate for mutual understanding. Cultures have to progress past a certain point in order to be welcome in galactic society. In "Glory," two Amalgam scientists go to a planet that has not yet made contact, where two dominant nations are locked in a Cold War–style conflict. The Amalgam researchers are perfectly honest about themselves and their mission—no Star Trek "Prime Directive" subterfuge here—but they are also honest about the fact that they will not share any particularly advanced technology with a culture that is still largely warlike.

There is also a question as to what duty we owe to creatures we did not create but cannot yet talk to. The disembodied explorers of *Diaspora* face this question as they set out to explore the galaxy, looking for something or someone who can help protect them from or prevent a potentially civilization-ending, extinction-level astrophysical cataclysm. Chapter 11 of the book is titled "Wang's Carpets," and as a stand-alone short story in slightly modified form this is one of Egan's most reprinted stories. It has appeared in Year's Best collections and also in SF anthologies such as *The Hard SF Renaissance* and *The Mammoth Book of Extreme SF*. The viewpoint character wakes up as the small ship that houses this incarnation of him orbits Vega; the ship reports that one of the planets there, Orpheus, is covered in water and shows signs of having life. So far, the probes have done their surveying from low orbit. The next step involves sending microprobes into the ocean, and that requires a two-thirds vote from the people onsite. At first, all they know is that there are "carpets" floating in the oceans that may be something like kelp forests. The first debate is between those who assert that the probes are extremely unlikely to do any harm, or even to be noticed, and those who point out that there is likewise no harm in waiting a few centuries or so to see what happens without interference (a lot of urgency can be removed from the equation when everyone is functionally immortal). The conservative faction pleads ignorance (not knowing what the consequences of contact will be, even though no one can elucidate a scenario in which the microprobes cause any harm), and the explorer faction points out that closer probing is the only way to solve the problem of ignorance. There might be rare tsunamis that could dump large amounts of organic matter on what shorelines exist—that would be easier and less obtrusive to study—but no one knows when such a jackpot would come about. Of course, they do not have truly unlimited time: there is the fear of galactic catastrophes and more mundane threats, such as meteorites. The vote is taken and the microprobes are launched.

As the data come in, the carpets become even more fascinating. For one thing, they are composed of a single, hugely macroscopic molecule instead of being a collection of molecules joined together like the forms of life we know. "It was a *single molecule*, a two-dimensional polymer weighing twenty-five thousand tons" (*Diaspora* 171). The carpets grow by adding new atoms at their edges, and divide when the mechanical wave action of the ocean breaks up the larger sheets. They come to be called Wang's carpets after Hao Wang, a real mathematician, 1921–1995, whose description of a certain kind of tile arrangement describes the carpet's growth pattern. Specifically, Wang posited the existence of a class of tiles that is equivalent to a universal Turing machine, that is, a computer capable of running programs.

Luckily, the probes have not harmed this unique life form, the only living thing on the planet. That's very interesting at first, but also a little disappointing. Everyone was hoping for creatures to converse with, but further examination reveals something nevertheless fascinating: the Wang's carpets are essentially living computers that can calculate or simulate anything, given enough time and space to do so. When they look at what the carpet is actually simulating, they discover a multidimensional space teeming with life forms. Although these carpets seem to drift aimlessly on an endless sterile ocean, inside their computational universe is an ocean as diverse as any coral reef on Earth, and Egan's description of these sixteen-dimensional life forms is lush and vivid. It also appears that the life there is conscious, but there is no way to contact or communicate with the creatures, as they are isolated within the simulations of their accidental biological computer system. In the end, the planet is left to its otherwise passive inhabitants, and the characters scatter in search of other worlds to explore, still hoping to find life out there to talk to.

It is no wonder that "Wang's Carpets" received so much acclaim, even as a short story. It is packed full of a sense of wonder, with everything from the incredibly novel aliens in the carpets to all the embodiment/virtuality/personality choices made by the "human" characters in space. One of the beautiful aspects of the story is that it takes something that most people would regard as "unnatural"—simulating life inside some sort of computer, especially life that is experienced in more dimensions than the four that we are accustomed to—and shows how such life could possibly come to exist through purely "natural" or "organic" means. It is aimed directly at the core of what many readers love about science fiction, a shot of pure, thoughtful wonderment. As one reviewer wrote: "This is hard science fiction as it is meant to be: no rayguns or warp drives, but ten-dimensional grand unified theories, the rotational dynamics of binary neutron stars and high level particle physics instead" (Anders Sandberg).

There is one instance in Egan's fiction where a first-contact situation immediately turns hostile, thanks in part to the blundering ignorance of one side. In the first of a linked pair of stories, "Luminous" and "Dark Integers," a small team of mathematicians finds out that the basic rules of math are not consistent across all of the real numbers. Imagine that the value of pi is different somewhere, billions of light years away on the far side of the universe—a proposition that may not be purely fanciful (Burnham *Clarkesworld*). This is analogous to the situation in these stories: the rules of mathematics are different for astronomically large numbers; in other words, if you try to perform a simple mathematical operation like addition on a ridiculously large number, you will find that you get a different answer than you expect from our "normal" math. For example, with these numbers, if $x + 1 = y + 1$, x and y are not necessarily equal. This started out as a thought experiment among graduate students, who then wrote some code to find out if any of these anomalous regions existed. It turns out that they do, and that there are other beings for whom that mathematical set of rules represents the normal workings of their universe. Conflict immediately ensues when it turns out that the investigations from "our side" of the boundary between the two rule sets are causing more of "their territory" to turn into "our territory" (our rules replacing theirs) accidentally. The far-side aliens immediately retaliate until communications are established and hostilities cease.

In the sequel, another researcher from our side blunders into the far-side space, causing damage. This time, the far-siders retaliate on a massive scale, causing anything on our side that relies on simple mathematical computations—for example, every digital computer ever built—to begin malfunctioning. Mathematical combat ensues until both sides agree to fortify the border such that neither side should be able to broach it again. These stories, unlike most of Egan's work, are structured as thrillers, with pure mathematicians placed in the heroic position of having to defend humanity from alien threats. There is a definite whiff of the Cold War about the stories. However, they share two features with other Egan stories: competing universal rules, and alternate universes that have much richer life than our own. We see the first scenario in the climax of stories such as *Permutation City*, when the Lambertians force the Elysians out of their created universe, and it is the plot driver of *Schild's Ladder*, as the novum converts our space at a prodigious rate. *Distress* also features this sort of conflict, through the fanciful construct of anthrocosmology (see chapter 4). The second point also comes through clearly in *Schild's Ladder*, as the novum universe has more life in its outer millimeter than an entire galaxy does in our universe.

Consider also the richness of the life inside the multidimensional space of Wang's carpets. It is a neat way of reminding readers that our "normal" universe may not be the best (or at least most life-friendly) of all possible worlds, and that the rules and scenarios we think of as "normal" and "natural" may be no more than a fluke.

When it comes to first-contact scenarios in Egan's fiction, the basic rule is: if it's intelligent, talk to it, and talk to it honestly. The only ethical course is to try to present all the facts so that both sides have the same understanding of the situation, at which point everyone can act as equal beings with equal rights. When it comes to life created by humans, even if it is software based instead of organic, it is important not to inflict pain and suffering on any conscious being. (In one of his early SF horror stories, "The Demon's Passage," Egan even has a laboratory animal speak up against its own suffering, although that suffering has resulted in its intelligence and ability to communicate.) Ideally, if we cannot communicate with a life form, we should leave it alone, as with Wang's carpets. However, when forced into conflict as in *Schild's Ladder* and "Dark Integers," the best bet is to find a compromise—almost nothing needs to be a zero-sum game. Overall, this reinforces the view of Egan's fiction as promoting a deeply humanist worldview tinged with a certain amount of optimism. His stories show a moral universe where the suffering of conscious beings should be avoided at all costs—even when those beings are "simulated"—and they dramatize the choices and consequences that derive from following that highest standard.

Chapter 3

IDENTITY AND CONSCIOUSNESS

Throughout Greg Egan's career, some of his strongest stories have focused on the theme of identity. This takes several forms, from the neurochemical components of identity in today's humans, through the identity shift as we make the transition into digital immortal beings, to the identity concerns unique to those digital descendants. When Egan's fiction takes up the question of identity it generally looks under the skin at the neural system of the brain. There are many questions about neurons and consciousness that science is only now beginning to answer—and the answers provided so far diverge wildly from our day-to-day perceptions of being.

NEUROCHEMICAL CONSCIOUSNESS

"Axiomatic" (1990) is a story from early in Egan's career that considers how much a brain can change and still maintain a consistent sense of self. It appeared in *Interzone* only four issues after "Learning to Be Me," which covers similar territory while dealing with technologically mediated consciousness. "Axiomatic" was chosen as the title story for Egan's first short story collection, and it is emblematic of his treatment of these themes throughout the 1990s.

It starts with a first-person narrator, who gives his name as Mark Carver, heading into an Implant Shop to buy a brain implant. He browses the racks of options, with categories such as MEDITATION AND HEALING and LANGUAGES AND TECHNICAL SKILLS, and titles such as *You are Great!* and *Love Yourself a Billion*. These implants can instantly give you a set of skills, such as a new language, or they can provide you with an unshakeable belief system, everything from Amish to Zen. "There was even an implant called *Secular Humanist* ('You WILL hold these truths to be self-evident!')" (*Axiomatic* 111). They are reversible: remove the implant, remove the belief system. Axioms are mathematical statements that are assumed to be true and cannot be questioned from within a particular mathematical system. In this story, you can make yourself axiomatically gay or straight, grant yourself a specific sexual fetish, or give yourself synaesthesia. The implant technology has the potential to veer into creepy mind-control territory, but Carver repeatedly emphasizes that simply changing your beliefs does not affect your free will. You choose the implant, and you choose what to do with the new beliefs that you have. In much the same way that someone who likes chocolate need not eat chocolate with every meal, simply neurochemically adopting a belief system like Catholicism doesn't force you to become a martyr or inquisitor.

The implant that Carver wants has to be specially ordered, and he is worried sick about it. His wife was killed in a bank hold-up five years previously, and he has been obsessed with her memory and the knowledge that her killer, positively identified as Patrick Anderson, got a light sentence for selling out his accomplices and is now walking free. Carver is a pacifist and an activist against the death penalty; he knows that Anderson has done his time and that nothing will bring back his wife. However, he has not been able to move on and is looking for an implant that will help him to do this. He has already (legally) bought a gun and joined a firing range, and (illegally, but with only a fine as a potential penalty) bought vaporizing ammunition and a silencer. He absolutely believes that killing is wrong. The brain implant he has ordered is titled "Life is cheap."

He sets the implant to be active for three days. With the knowledge that he could stop at any time, knowing that his wife is dead and nothing he does can affect her, that she would be horrified at what he's thinking of doing, that he could be caught—but without any particular feeling that killing is wrong—he puts the gun in his pocket and heads to Anderson's house. He continually interrogates himself—why am I doing this? Over and over he raises self-justifying possibilities and then discards them before finally deciding, "I had to accept the unpleasant fact that I honestly wanted to kill Anderson, and however much I had also been repelled by the notion, to be true to myself I had to do it—anything less would have been hypocrisy and self-deception" (*Axiomatic* 120).

He ambushes Anderson and takes the opportunity to ask him repeatedly why he killed his wife. In the end the most honest answer Anderson has is: "I lost my temper, all right? Things were going badly, and I lost my fucking temper, and there she was, all right?" (*Axiomatic* 123). Drawing on his own experience of lashing out in petty frustration and armed with the "Life is cheap" implant, Carver recognizes this as being absolutely true, and it is the only explanation for his wife's death that he will ever get. And blissfully, he doesn't care. His wife's life was as cheap as any other. As Anderson springs at him Carver shoots him dead, then calmly walks away.

At the end of the story, he returns to the Implant Shop to buy a permanent implant to replace the temporary one he had used.

> This time, I know exactly what I want.
>
> What I want is what I felt that night: the unshakeable conviction that Amy's death—let alone Anderson's—simply didn't matter. . . . My one mistake was thinking that the insight I gained would simply vanish when the implant cut out. It hasn't. It's been clouded with doubts and reservations . . . but I can still recall the peace it gave me . . . having tasted the freedom of certainty, I find I can't live without it. . . . Part of me, of course, still finds the prospect of what I am about to do totally repugnant.
>
> No matter. That won't last. (*Axiomatic* 124)

The same brain implant technology appears in "The Walk." The first-person narrator has crossed a mob financier and is taken out into the woods to be executed by a hit man. The narrator pleads for his life, but instead the hit man offers him a neural implant that should make him feel better about dying. The implant confers the belief that out of all the humans who exist throughout all of time, statistically speaking, one of them will be just like you. So it's OK that you die—the essence of "you" will recur somewhere, somewhen. It is almost like reincarnation for atheists. The victim takes the implant and tells the hit man that while he is still afraid to die, he can finally accept it—at which point the hit man kills himself instead of the intended victim. The story does not work terribly well: because we never get the point of view of the hit man, we have no idea why he decides to kill himself. In fact, having heard what he needs to from the victim, it seems that he could have killed the victim, lived many more years, and then offed himself with aplomb at some later point in his life. But once again we are presented with the idea that changing the hardwiring in our brains in order to force a set of beliefs onto it does not change our individual free will.

Egan's first SF novel, *Quarantine* (1992), tangentially touches on the same issues, although the technology takes a different form. While the plot of *Quarantine* focuses on how human consciousness may interact with quantum wave functions, the protagonist Nick lives in a near future that shares some aspects with "Axiomatic." When Nick worked as a police officer, he took daily neurochemicals, or "priming mods," of which there are different versions that would make him supremely unemotional and focused on his job. Theoretically, they would wear off after a shift and he would be able to go home and be "normal." When his wife dies in a terrorist bombing, he essentially decides to remain on those chemicals forever rather than deal with the emotional toll that he knows will come. He becomes a private detective (an SF trope with a long and honorable tradition), and while on a case he is eventually captured by the bad guys, a conglomerate known as the Ensemble. Instead of killing Nick, they give him a brain mod that makes him unshakably loyal to the Ensemble, and he is given guard duties in one of their research labs. There he learns a great deal about their research into quantum states and consciousness before eventually joining together with others in the same situation as he is in to think their way around the constraints imposed by the loyalty mod.

Two lesser stories also touch upon the same theme: "Mister Volition" and "Steve Fever." "Steve Fever" involves a brain virus that co-opts people as it tries to fulfil its mission to somehow recreate the scientist, named Steve, who created it. It is a classic unintended-consequences-of-technology story, with the collective intelligence of the brain virus depicted as a bumbling, incompetent, please-don't-accidentally-step-on-me sort of overlord. The tale is mostly satirical, aimed at those who believe that bootstrapped computers may turn into a benign super-overlord AI that will fix all our problems. But there is still the question of the boy who gets caught up in the Steveware's latest plan: "So what was his role now? Traitor? Double agent? Prisoner of war? People talked about sleepwalkers and zombies, but in truth there was still no right word for what he had become" ("Steve Fever" 5). "Mister Volition," in common with "The Walk," features a criminal with philosophical tendencies. He is obsessed with free will and the fact that all his choices are his own. "I need not choose violence, but my choices are meaningless if they're encumbered by social mores and sentimentality, hypocrisy and self-delusion" (*Luminous* 107). When he steals an eye-patch implant, designed for bio-feedback, that displays his own brain back to him in real time, he becomes obsessed with visualizing the "I" that makes the decisions—that part of his brain that "is" his free will in some sense. He labels this hypothetical golem inside the brain "Mister Volition." He picks a victim and aims to shoot him, because he can and because he wants to see the choice being made. But in truth (backed up by medicine's current understanding of neural function), there is no single "I" in the brain—it is a post hoc fiction that humans use to rationalize a choice made all over the brain before we are conscious of making it. This realization sends the narrator into a vertiginous paroxysm of understanding the base materiality of existence—there is no "soul" animating the machine; the machine is all we are. In the story notes for "Mister Volition" in *Luminous*, Egan points interested readers to the ideas of Marvin Minsky (*The Society of Mind*) and Daniel C. Dennett (*Consciousness Explained*) for explanations of the models of mind that he dramatizes here.

Taking an even stranger premise, "The Safe-Deposit Box" looks at the difficulties of constructing an identity when one's life is the opposite of normal. The narrator of this story never wakes up in the same body two days in a row. While the bodies he wakes up in are all males of the same age living in a bounded geographical region, there is no continuity in his life from one day to the next. It has been this way since he can remember—as he was growing up, it took him a long time to realize that other people's families and houses didn't change every morning. He has gotten entirely used to working out who he is meant to be each day by checking the clues of each life—wallet, ID badges, uniforms, evidence of wives and children, and so on. He also keeps notes that he leaves himself in a safe-deposit box in a central location each day; that is how he discovered that all his hosts live in a single city. In the story he comes close to solving the mystery of why he was born this way, something rather implausible to do with extreme parental abuse by a neuroscientist. This, along with "Unstable Orbits in the Space of Lies," is just about as non-scientific as Egan gets.

The most interesting part of the story has to do with how the man stays sane and constructs his own sense of self. Most of the men he becomes are middle-aged and heterosexual, hence married. It is easy for him to fall into the patterns of "being married," even though the details change each day. Similarly it is easy to match each day to the stereotype of "going to work" and "bantering with co-workers." He manages to cobble together an education through exposure to classrooms, and, more important, through his own reading. "Had I 'grown up' in bodies of completely random ages, or in hosts scattered worldwide, with a different language and culture to contend with every day, I doubt that I'd even *exist*—no personality could possibly emerge from such a cacophony of experiences. (Then again, an ordinary person might think the same of my own, relatively stable, origins)" (*Axiomatic* 127–28). But it bothers him immensely that he does not have a name of his own, and never will.

These stories, along with "Seeing" (original to *Axiomatic*) illustrate just how alien our brains really are compared to our experience of living and thinking. "Seeing" reads rather like an Oliver Sacks case study. The narrator has been shot in the head and begins to experience vision as if he were floating above his body in a sort of permanent out-of-body experience. It is a phenomenon similar to the more famous concept of blindsight: "where people lose all sense of visual awareness but they can still guess what's in front of them, if they really try, because the information is still coming through" (*Luminous* 94). Here, Egan is working in territory that has also been profitably explored by SF writers such as Daryl Gregory and Peter Watts. Gregory is perhaps best known for his much-anthologized story "Second Person, Present Tense" in which a drug overdose causes a teenage girl to become, in effect, a completely different person from her past self. She has all the memories of her original self, but no emotional connection to them. She believes herself to be an entirely new person, and she wants a new name and to be treated as who she has become. Understandably, her parents are horrified, and the novelette is a moving family drama. Peter Watts, a Canadian marine biologist, writes books that have been described as "hard biological SF" and "hard psychological SF." One of his most noted works is the Hugo-nominated novel *Blindsight*, in which a team of deliberately chosen, uniquely brain-damaged individuals (brain-damaged in ways that optimize different aspects of their performance) are sent to meet an alien threat. At least some of the aliens are intelligent but not sentient in any way we understand the term—the novel argues that consciousness and sentience are evolutionary flukes that may not be necessary or even advantageous.

Along with "Learning to Be Me," the other story Egan has identified as a personal favorite is "Reasons to Be Cheerful" (1997), which is also a story of neurological damage. As a boy of twelve, for no particular reason, the narrator becomes 100 percent happy with his life. He simply always feels happy about the way things are going, and minor setbacks never significantly affect his mood. It turned out that this is the effect of a brain tumor, which is eventually removed. However, as a consequence of the surgery, the boy loses the ability to feel any pleasure in anything at all. Absolutely nothing can make him happy. Needless to say, this makes it almost impossible for him to live a normal life. The story then jumps ahead roughly fifteen years, and the scene opens: "The alarm woke me up then, but it took me another three hours to summon up the energy to move. . . . *Nothing helps, nothing changes*. Four words said it all" (*Luminous* 223). He is supported by an insurance company for his untreatable medical condition, but what he lives is barely a life. All drugs can do is rescue him from catatonia, not actually give him the ability to feel pleasure. He is offered an experimental therapy involving a neural prosthesis. And it works—to an extent. He can feel pleasure again but with no discrimination. In order for him to return to normality, a user interface is designed for him so that he can choose what things make him happy and how happy they will make him. All his pleasure triggers are under his direct control. He now possesses the opportunity to tailor his own nervous system to create a happy, healthy life—no trivial task, and indeed in some ways a curse.

One of the key strengths of these stories is that through the use of first-person narrators, Egan deftly relates to us the *experience* of living with abnormal-to-the-point-of-alien neurological conditions. This ability to get inside the minds of characters far different from ourselves also comes in handy when the brains involved run on software instead of organic brains. Egan is frequently criticized for poor characterization, but as he put it in a 1993 interview:

> I think my stories work best when there's a powerful reason for the idea to be important to the central character. Most of my characters are a bit obsessive, and a bit fucked-up—but I'd rather that than have them scrupulously bland and ordinary for the sake of it. . . .
>
> A complicating factor is that a lot of my work is aimed at undermining orthodox ideas about personal identity, so it's hardly the place you'd expect to find the usual nineteenth-century literary conventions about characterisation being honoured. Emma Bovary couldn't pop out and buy the neural implant from "Fidelity."
>
> None of that's meant to be an excuse for poor writing—and I know I have a long way to go in a lot of areas. I'm sure I've had stories published which have been successful because the ideas were strong enough for readers to forgive a degree of clumsiness in the style and the characterisation. Obviously, I'd rather have everything work together. I want to improve on those fronts—without sacrificing the ideas. ("Burning the Motherhood Statements")

DIGITAL CONSCIOUSNESS

The next set of identity concerns arise when we seek to immortalize our brains using some form of digital technology. One of Egan's earliest and most important stories along these lines is "Learning to Be Me" (1990). It opens with one of those gosh-wow SF lines: "I was six years old when my parents told me that there was a small, dark jewel inside my skull, learning to be me" (*Axiomatic* 185). The technology is an artificial neural net that is implanted in the brain and grows along with it. Neural nets are "trained" by taking input, providing output, and then comparing that output to some objective. Whenever the output is "wrong" compared to the objective, the neural net is tweaked slightly. Whenever the output is "right," its configuration is reinforced. The idea in the story is that the neural net receives all the sensory data input the original brain receives and then compares its output to what the brain actually does. After many years of perfecting itself (usually around age thirty) the organic brain is removed and the neural net (the "jewel") is made fully operational. The user should be confident that it will act exactly as the original brain would have acted. This is the best possible scenario for using a neural network design to mimic human brain function; usually, neural networks are created for more limited applications since the input/output data and time for training is highly constrained.

Critically, the story has a first-person narrator, unnamed. Growing up in a society where the jewels are common, he wrestles with the thought of it, through schoolboy jokes, philosophical musings, relationship arguments (he leaves his wife rather than go through the transition with her), and he briefly joins an anti-jewel conspiracy group. He vacillates between assuming that the jewel really is a perfect mirror of one's consciousness and the nagging suspicion that any mechanical analog of a brain cannot be truly human. The arguments reflect debates about AIs as well as philosophical debates about other intangibles such as the incorporeal soul. After years of obsessing over the issue, he finally decides to schedule the switching surgery, as much out of exhaustion as for any other reason.

The critical moment comes some months before the surgery when the narrator suddenly loses control of his body—he wants to do one thing, but he watches his body do something else instead. It starts with a trivial matter, wanting to order an apple during online grocery shopping (in 1990, before America Online ever sent out a mass mailing CD) and watching his body order pineapples instead. He descends into panic while his body continues with its routine. At first he thinks that he has somehow spontaneously switched, that the jewel is now in control and he is trapped. However that couldn't happen without an army of medical nanobots. Instead, he comes to realize that "he," the narrator, is the jewel. The training function has gone awry such that he is no longer in line with the organic original, but his "output" is still disconnected from the body's functions. He and his original are drifting apart, becoming different people.

This causes another round of panic—the surgery procedure is supposed to be preceded by a test of the jewel versus organic functioning. If he is no longer mimicking the original perfectly, it should be detected and he (the jewel) will be shut down rather than have an imperfect copy replace the organic brain.

He wants to survive, but the separation is increasing by the day. The original has fallen in love with a woman for whom the jewel narrator feels nothing.

When the operation is over, the narrator wakes up. He sees the new girlfriend, reassuring him that he is the same person he has always been. But now he knows the answers to all his questions. He knows that the jewel is fully capable of all the depth and richness of human experience. But he also knows that it is not the same person as the organic brain that dies. And he knows that the checks and balances of the medical profession are mere voiced pieties, ignored when the reality becomes too messy. The sense of dislocation and existential vertigo are profound, all in a story with an unnamed and undescribed protagonist, and with only three named characters who have no physical descriptions to differentiate one from another.

Egan revisited this technology twice, in "Closer" (1992) and "Border Guards" (1999). "Border Guards" has more to do with humanity's dislocation in becoming immortal, as well as the lasting effects of trauma. In "Closer" the protagonist Michael switches over to the jewel happily and without reservations—he has always identified with the jewel, and he sees the embryonic organic brain as merely a disposable part of his lifecycle. Instead, his obsession is: "I desperately wanted to believe that other people are somehow *knowable*, but it wasn't something I could bring myself to take for granted" (*Axiomatic* 305). He echoes several other of Egan's romantically clueless protagonists when he says of his girlfriend, Sian: "For a start, I rarely had any idea what she was thinking—in the sense of knowing how she would have replied if asked, out of the blue, to describe her thoughts at the moment before they were interrupted by the question. On a longer timescale, I had no feeling for her motivation, her image of herself, her concept of who she was and what she did and why" (*Axiomatic* 308–09). Nonetheless, they are happy together at the start of their immortal lives.

As the technology develops to allow them to become more personally adventurous, they start to explore the question of getting closer to "knowing" another person. As Sian says, "If we really are going to live forever, we'd better stay curious if we want to stay sane" (*Axiomatic* 310). They go through the various permutations of bodyswapping: him in her body, she in his, both transitioning to become hermaphroditic identical twins. Finally, they sign up with a researcher who promises to blend their consciousnesses (based on their jewel devices) and implant them in identical robot bodies for eight hours, then restore their original jewel configurations but with the memory of the experience. For the eight hours in the robot bodies, they will be functionally identical people, and afterward they will have the most perfect "shared" experience possible. As the story recounts the eight hours in the robot body, the story falters in that the personality describing the experience does not seem fundamentally different from Michael's, which means that the whole section lacks the sort of cognitive dissonance that features in "Learning to Be Me." And it ends with an anticlimax as, after their personalities are once again separated, Michael and Sian break up—not because they found anything scandalous in their understanding of each other, but more because they now find each other desperately boring. They have no sense of *otherness* in dealing with each other and thus find little interest in spending eternity together. This is in contrast to "Learning to Be Me," in which two personalities (the original and the jewel) become drastically divergent after only a short time, despite having spent decades in enforced lockstep. Michael and Sian diverge after their shared experience, but not enough to make them interesting to each other.

The other method for "normal" humans to achieve digital immortality provides the basis for *Permutation City* and stories such as "Transition Dreams" and "A Kidnapping." A human being is scanned, and the Copy wakes up in a virtual reality. At the beginning of *Permutation City* a Copy of Paul Durham wakes up and immediately tries to commit suicide—no matter how good the simulation is, knowing that he is stuck in a simulation (running much slower than real time) while a flesh and blood version of himself walks around in the real world is too much for him to bear. We learn that while Copies of terminally ill or deceased persons are usually content to accept their fate, Copies of young healthy people "bail-out" at a rate of 100 percent, especially in the early days when the simulations are very limited and there are few people to talk to. The only way Durham keeps his "Copy" alive is through a feat of technological and ethical sleight of hand.

Durham's Copy grudgingly embarks on experimentation with different ways of running the software that is his consciousness. Subjectively, it does not make any difference to him if he is run on fast computers or slow ones, or if one hundred steps in calculating his reality are run on one hundred separate servers and only combined at the end. Pausing and restarting, running backward or out of order—it all ultimately leads to the same subjective experience.

All four viewpoint characters of *Permutation City* are obsessive personalities to a greater or lesser extent. Durham is obsessed with the experience of digital consciousness, and also with ensuring his digital immortality regardless of his eventual purchasing power for computer time. Thomas Riemann is a billionaire industrialist who subjects his digital copy to an eternal hell as partial expiation for his sin in killing his lover in his youth, something for which he has never been able to forgive himself. Peer is the digital embodiment of a man who was once David Hawthorne—following Hawthorne's death in an accident, his estate could only afford the slowest, cheapest amount of computer time to run his Copy. He is disillusioned by so quickly losing touch with the outside world. However, together with other Copies in the same situation, he has embarked on a grand experiment of self-editing—making it easy to pass the time by programming himself to enjoy all sorts of repetitive tasks. When we meet him he has been climbing down the outside of an infinite skyscraper, gecko-style, for a large amount of subjective time. "[H]e'd edited out any need or desire for food, drink, sleep, sex, companionship, or even a change in scenery. . . . He resumed the descent gladly, a happy Sisyphus" (*Permutation City* 61). Interestingly, one constant of his personality that he chooses to leave intact, one of his very few touchstones, is his relationship with and attraction to Kate, the first Copy to reach out to him in his diminished initial-waking state. It is an odd but perfectly legitimate choice to partly define oneself by one's relationship to another. People do this all the time (imagine how much individuals change throughout, say, fifty years of marriage, all the while defining that relationship as a critical part of themselves), but it is interesting to see it as a conscious choice in a personality otherwise so radically plastic.

In this company, Maria seems almost normal—she has a hobby that she really enjoys, and she spends probably a bit too much of her free time and money on it. She's playing around in a computerized environment called the Autoverse that has a very simple set of rules (simplified analogs of the laws of physics for our universe), but those can give rise to surprising amounts of complexity. She's been working on creating self-sustaining entities that could be the equivalent of life, a field known as Artificial Life (as opposed to Artificial Intelligence). When Paul Durham comes along, she is willing to accept his offer of computing resources to complete her hobbyist project. Eventually, Copies of all these characters come to exist in a sort of infinite and self-perpetuating pocket universe permanently divorced from our universe. The final third of the book extrapolates that universe and its society after several thousand years of subjective time. This may be the weakest part of the book, as Gary Wolfe mentioned in his *Locus* review: "We get a bunch of aging neurotics who seem to have no idea at all what to do with an almost infinitely malleable universe" (Wolfe 23).

Permutation City is Egan's most sustained focus on the experience of digital consciousness as it compares to our own experience; being set mostly in the near future, it invites those direct comparisons. In *Diaspora*, *Schild's Ladder*, and *Incandescence*, the characters exist so far into the future that they take digital consciousness for granted—for them, infinitely malleable digital landscapes, communities formed around shared preferences for communications protocols, and the ability to edit yourself and change your embodiment are all matter-of-fact and mundane realities.

This point is repeated many times in Egan's stories: we change at every minute of every day but our perception of consciousness is designed to paper over these changes. Neurons die, synaptic connections are strengthened and weakened. Experiences are remembered or forgotten. We can lose skin cells without noticing, neurons without perceiving; entire organs can be replaced, even major brain damage can leave a person coherent and functional. It is the rare stroke that changes a person's sense of self (although such things are possible). So why wouldn't we instinctively maintain that sense of continuity if we grew up changing bodies daily, or transitioned to an immortal neural network, or ran on computer servers scattered across the globe? The change between the original brain and the jewel of the narrator in "Learning to Be Me" is arguably less drastic than the change in one individual between ages fifteen and thirty, or even between one person before and after a traumatic event. If consciousness can survive everything that biology throws at it, there may be little to fear when looking to upload our brains in the future.

Rather than continuity, one thing that does worry some of Egan's protagonists is choice. If one accepts the (still controversial) many-worlds interpretation (MWI) of quantum physics, then every "choice" in the universe causes new worlds representing all possible outcomes to branch off from the original timeline. This event can be something microscopic, such as a photon of light going through one of two slits, or something macroscopic, such as the decision to intervene in a violent beating, as in Egan's 2002 story, "Singleton." Fundamentally, then, any choice you make could be considered irrelevant, since at least some universe has you making every possible version of that choice. If we accept MWI as true, then this is the truth of our everyday reality. Obviously no one acts as if this is true, since there are any number of consequences that come from "bad" choices. But Ben, the narrator of "Singleton," is obsessed (continuing a trend in Egan's protagonists) with the idea that MWI renders choice meaningless—that for every "you" that gets something right, a huge number of "you" get it wrong and have to live with that. His wife agrees that MWI has perfectly reasonable physics and agrees that it implies that there are an infinite number of "her" in other branches, but she takes the more pragmatic philosophy that it has nothing to do with her and has no impact on her choices. Still, there is a reason humans place more moral weight on the decision of a free person to act compared to a roll of a die. If all roads are taken, is one wise to have chosen a good road, or merely lucky to be the "one" version that does so?

Quantum computers take advantage of quantum mechanical effects to compute complex calculations extremely quickly. While a normal computer runs on transistors that can only be in one state at a time (on or off, 0 or 1), a quantum computer can define a problem such that a number of states can exist simultaneously. While the field is still very new, progress toward functional quantum computers is proceeding rapidly. In "Singleton," Ben makes use of advanced quantum computing technology to create a "quantum singleton processor" or Qusp, a computer which uses quantum superposition but always arrives at a single, classically deterministic answer. Through shielding, it is prevented from spawning multiple worlds with every possible variation of the result. Ben runs this through a number of tests, and eventually he and his wife decide to use this system as the basis for raising an AI child. The child's brain is programmed into a Qusp and then loaded into a robotic body. The child, Helen, is allowed to grow from literal infancy to adulthood, with her body being upgraded along the way. At this point, in 2031, AI children are rare but becoming more common. Helen is unique in that unlike the other AIs and unlike normal humans, her choices always end in only one result on a quantum level. If she ever wanted to give up that difference, removing the special shielding on her Qusp would cause her to operate in a branching reality like everyone else. In the end, after a difficult adolescence, Helen says: "[W]hat I have is something almost every person who's ever lived thought they possessed. Human psychology, human culture, human morality, all evolved with the illusion that we lived in a single history. But we don't—so in the long run, something has to give. Call me old-fashioned, but I'd rather we tinker with our physical nature than abandon our whole identities" (*Crystal Nights and Other Stories* 184–85). Not everyone is as sanguine about the continuity of consciousness when making the transition to substances other than our organic brains, nor so worried about the moral implications of the many-worlds interpretation of quantum physics. Egan's range of stories shows a continuity of concern about these subjects that refuses superficial answers and instead examines them in depth.

CONSCIOUSNESS AS INFORMATION

The idea of digital immortality is part of a broader cultural conversation that has been developing over the past century (looked at in one way) and millennia (looked at in another). Stretching back to prehistory there has been a perception in some cultures, particularly Western ones, that some part of ourselves is separate from our bodies. Through most of human history this has been identified as an incorporeal soul that survives the death of the body and is then consigned to any number of imaginative fates. As science developed from the Greeks through the Enlightenment, the understanding of a materialist universe left less room for incorporeal, unobservable phenomena. Through the twentieth and early twenty-first centuries, the understanding of the universe as being materialistic has hardened (despite many cultural movements pushing against this trend). At the same time, science's understanding of the nature and material of the universe has become increasingly abstract. Consider that matter, seemingly the simplest stuff we deal with every day, is now known to consist mostly of empty space. When we interact with "solid" matter, what we are really experiencing is the product of the forces binding particles together. And even those particles and forces are not fully understood, with several theoretical candidates vying for the privilege of explaining their make-up and existence (with string theory currently the most famous hypothesis).

Another area of rapid advancement is the idea of information. Much of the history of the last 120 years or so can be seen through the lens of information, its definition, and its reproduction. Not for nothing do some label the past few decades the Information Age (with the delimiting years varying depending on the expert). On the one hand, computers and other information technology have made huge and rapid strides, transforming cultures all over the world. Transistors and integrated-circuit technology have made cheap, ubiquitous computing power available over wide swaths of the globe. Communication networks connect far-flung people and economies. At the same time, popular science and science-fictional concepts have shaped people's perceptions of the world. The discovery of DNA in the 1950s made it clear that information (for example, the four base pairs that make up the larger DNA molecule and encode our genetic information) is fundamental to our humanity and individuality. The teleporters in *Star Trek*, one of the most widely known science-fictional properties of all time, are based on the notion that humans can be broken down into streams of information, beamed across space, and reconstituted in a new place, without loss of flesh or consciousness (several dramatic teleporter mishaps notwithstanding). Androids such as Data from *Star Trek: The Next Generation* or those from the *Blade Runner* movie (based on Philip K. Dick's *Do Androids Dream of Electric Sheep?*) made people more comfortable with the idea of artificial intelligence achieving human status. Cyberpunk works showed humans interfacing directly with computers, which seemed all the more reasonable as computers and the internet became increasingly ubiquitous. Popular virtual realities and Massively Multiplayer Online Role Playing Games (MMORPGs) such as *World of Warcraft* make navigating artificial realities seem normal. All of this adds up to a significant segment of the world's population assuming that humanity's becoming digital is both possible and possibly a natural progression.

In this context, it makes sense to assume (as SF always assumes that the engineering will work out eventually) that we can build computers to simulate ourselves and other universes. At that point there is nothing restricting life to existing in conventional four-dimensional universes like our own. With even relatively simple number-crunching programs, scientists often simulate physical or mathematical systems that exist in many more dimensions than the four (up, forward, sideways, and time) dimensions we are familiar with. For instance, string theorists talk about subatomic particles being strings that are vibrating in ten or eleven (or more) dimensions. At the moment, there is no way that we know of for a human mind to visualize an object in five dimensions without resorting to various projections, although we can easily describe such things mathematically. In *Diaspora* the digitally simulated characters are able to alter their perceptions such that operating in five or more dimensions is perfectly intuitive. Because of the difficulty in describing this sort of environment in any useful way, most SF authors have eschewed that particular challenge.

As well as different dimensional space, Egan's fiction also imagines many different "platforms" for simulation than we typically think of. When we picture a simulation, we usually think of a computer made of silicon in a box somewhere, running code. However, almost any physical system can act as a computer when manipulated the right way. In *Diaspora* the "Wang's Carpets" chapter imagines life simulated in the sixteen-dimensional Fourier transforms of a gigantic molecule. A Fourier transform is a way of describing a signal and is most commonly seen in sound-recording studios. While a song may be recorded and played back as a sequential series of notes in time that we listen to, another way of displaying the same song is to analyze the frequencies of all the sounds present in the song and to show all those frequencies at once. This is simply a different way of displaying the same information. In "Wang's Carpets" the scientists encounter individual molecules each weighing more than twenty-five tons. While the molecules are "alive" and growing, they are certainly not sentient life. However, one of the posthuman characters, idly playing around with modeling software, models the molecules in terms of their Fourier transforms. In the sixteen-dimensional version the character sees that the equivalent of a computer program is running, and within that program is a vast and rich ecosystem, complete with identifiable individuals with all the properties of sentience (including self-awareness and awareness of others as sentient beings). This is an almost unfathomably alien concept of "life," but once we accept that sentient beings can be simulated and that many physical systems can behave like computers and run simulation programs, it becomes, if not intuitive, at least comprehensible. In that context, the stories "Luminous" and "Dark Integers," where intelligent beings exist in a region of alternate mathematics, out in the space of transastronomical numbers (numbers larger than the number of atoms in the universe, for instance), seem almost mundane. If we envision life as information, there is no end to the possibilities of where and how that life can arise.

Transhumanist organizations such as Humanity Plus (H+) take this to its current extreme. They advocate for any technology that can improve human existence—aiming to make us stronger, faster, smarter, and immortal, if possible. In pushing for human enhancements *right now*, they are part of the bleeding edge, posing questions that many people are not yet comfortable answering. For instance, while most people are comfortable using prosthetics to restore mobility to someone missing a leg, what about a prosthetic that would allow someone to run faster than an Olympic-level sprinter, a prospect which became much more feasible in the wake of Oscar Pistorius's appearance in the 2012 Summer Olympics. Most people react with revulsion at the idea of someone having their perfectly functional legs amputated in favor of "superior" prosthetics, but it is difficult to pinpoint a nonvisceral argument against it. So far, most of these debates are occurring in small, out-of-the-way venues such as special-interest blogs and academic journals. However, the time is probably coming when some of these debates will begin to play out in major cultural and governmental milieus.

Along these lines, many people are uncomfortable with the rather nonchalant assumption that humanity can move into the future as immortal digital beings. They question the basis on which these futures are predicted, the potential current and future consequences, and the unspoken assumptions that surround the ideas. N. Katherine Hayles's *How We Became Posthuman* is a thorough critique of the current understanding of information and how it has been absorbed into the larger culture. She looks back at the earliest days of cybernetics research and explains how our current understanding of information is not the only way it could be understood. Claude Shannon was a key figure in the early days of thinking about information, and he needed to think about it specifically to solve problems for the military in World War II and for Bell Labs, a division of AT&T. He was concerned with transmitting messages through physical wires in the presence of noisy interference. As such, he came up with a mathematical definition of information that is very different from the common usage of the term. In this strictly technical sense, information is unrelated to meaning. Instead, it is a measure of uncertainty related to entropy. Redundancy actually reduces information content. Under this formulation, a string of random coin flips carries more "information" than a Shakespearean sonnet, since the sonnet is filled with the redundancies encoded in human language. Other ways of defining information were proposed in the 1950s; for instance, Donald MacKay would have measured information by the effect it caused in the receiver. If this proposal had been adopted, the sonnet would carry more information when read by a human, and the random coin flips would yield more information when causing a machine to choose between two alternatives. However, especially with regard to the changes information might cause in a human brain, this was impossible to measure with the technology of the day (and would still be difficult and imprecise today). As such Shannon's version, in which information is independent of sender, receiver, transmission method, and meaning, won the day.

When looked at in this rather sterile, non-intuitive way, information is independent of the medium that carries it. One can send the message "Hello, World" by speaking it (either in person or on the phone), typing it directly onto paper, sending it via radio waves (either encoding the text or the sound of it being spoken), emailing, texting, semaphore, Morse code, ASCII code, or myriad other ways. In theory, "Hello, World" has the same information content regardless of the method of delivery. In terms of our experience as human beings communicating, this is only partly true. It makes a big difference if a friend speaking to you face to face says "Hello, World" (Is she saying it ironically? Humorously? Sincerely?) or perhaps sends you an email with that message (Testing out a new system? Private joke? Cheerful greeting?) or stands at the end of the street waving semaphore flags (???). This is perhaps one of the fundamental disconnects between those envisioning a smooth transition to simulating humans as digital consciousness and those who feel that it will never be the same as physical existence.

Part of Hayles's critique comes down to the statement: "The technological processes involved in this transformation [for example, typesetting a book] are not neutral" (Hayles 28). A large number of studies have shown that this is true. Anecdotally, many authors find that they write differently when they write longhand in pen compared to typing on a computer. Study after study has shown that people interact with information differently according to how it is presented: a classroom compared to a TV show, one's parents compared to one's friends, newspaper compared to radio, even the font in which text is displayed makes a difference in people's absorption and acceptance of information. Expanding these objections to digitizing consciousness is obvious—there is a lot scientists do not know about how our brains work. Even things that are well established, such as neuron firings, are simplifications that do not explain all the behavior of the brain. In addition, brains are embedded in a complex biological feedback system that includes sensory input, proprioception, hormone levels, and other neurochemicals. No model of the brain that exists today adequately accounts for all the variables that affect its functioning. Given all this, Hayles asks on the first page of *How We Became Posthuman*: "How . . . was it possible for someone . . . to believe that mind could be separated from body? Even assuming such a separation was possible, how could anyone think that consciousness in an entirely different medium would remain unchanged, as if it had no connection with embodiment?"

Egan responded to this sort of critique when he commented on a blog post by Russell Blackford, "Transhumanism Still at the Crossroads":

> If you're just stressing the point that the human mind is a product of a vast biological, evolutionary and social context, and can't be understood in isolation from that context, I agree with you 100%. But all except the most naive notions of uploading include some effort to reproduce that context, and in the limiting case of sufficiently far-future technology, there is no physical principle to prevent the uploading of everything which is capable of having a causal effect on a given person's brain, body and behaviour. In that limit we could even satisfy Roger Penrose and simulate everything (a person's whole body and immediate environment, down to the atomic level) on a quantum computer.
>
> To render the most sophisticated forms of uploading impossible for all time, you really have to insist that *only the precise biochemistry of the human brain* can give rise to human subjective experience—or if you accept some level of substitutions, you need to offer some basis on which certain substitutions leave our experience intact, while others don't.
>
> [. . .]
>
> For example, Hans Moravec asks us to think about what we believe would happen if we replaced various proportions of our central nervous system with prosthetic subsystems that were capable of producing the same biochemical outputs from the same inputs. Does 1 prosthetic neuron stop me being me? Stop me being human? Stop me being conscious? How about 10, 100, etc.? (Blackford 2008)

Hans Moravec has been involved in artificial intelligence and robotics research since the 1970s and has worked to popularize his vision of robots and AIs in the future. His name is associated with intelligent robotics to the extent that in Dan Simmons's far-future duology, *Ilium* and *Olympos*, the robots darting around the solar system—charming viewpoint characters in their own right—are called "moravecs." Chapter 4 of Moravec's book *Mind Children: The Future of Robot and Human Intelligence* (1988) lays out in nonfictional form the ideas that establish the basis for many of Egan's stories from the 1990s: sending humans into space (expensive and dangerous) versus sending self-repairing machines (cheaper and easier) (*Diaspora*); scanning a brain to transfer it to a computer (*Permutation City*); comparing the new brain's function to the original and having an implanted computer that learns from the organic brain ("Learning to Be Me"); having a computer recording all your information such that when you die you can be restored (*Schild's Ladder*); having widely dispersed copies of yourself, running faster or slower depending on resources (*Permutation City*); sending robotic scouts out to space, having them build computers, then transmitting your information to that computer (*Schild's Ladder*); editing your capacity for boredom (*Permutation City*); merging information from different copies into one ("Closer"); and others. This slim volume of nonfiction reads like a rapid-fire summary of the plots of a library's worth of science fiction stories.

Moravec addresses a particular concern about brain uploading: "Regardless of how the copying is done, the end result will be a new person. If it is I who am being copied, the copy, though it may think of itself as me, is simply a self-deluded impostor. If the copying process destroys the original, then I have been killed" (Moravec 116). ("Learning to Be Me," of course, is told from the viewpoint of that self-deluded impostor.) Moravec suggests that the concern arises from identifying oneself with one's body, and he proposes a cognitive shift to identifying oneself with the pattern (information) that is present in the brain, independent of the brain itself. He specifically calls out teleporters ("matter transmitters") as a way of making people comfortable with the thought process. Of course, when it comes to the idea of digital immortality, there are many more criticisms to be addressed.

In *Unbearable Weight: Feminism, Western Culture, and the Body* (1993) Susan Bordo sees a cultural tendency toward body loathing in the project to see the world as information and leave the body behind. Bordo points out that in the Western/Christian tradition, "what remains the constant element throughout historical variation is the *construction* of body as something apart from the true self (whether conceived as soul, mind, spirit, will, creativity, freedom . . .) and as undermining the best efforts of that self. That which is not-body is the highest, the best, the noblest, the closest to God; that which is body is the albatross, the heavy drag on self-realization" (5). The idea of bodies as information and constructed texts permeates academic theories as well. Feminist scholars such as Judith Butler describe the biological body as being forever "historically and politically 'inscribed' and shaped" (qtd. in Bordo 288). When one sees the body as "text" that can be interpreted and rewritten, that makes virtual embodiment seem all the more appropriate and plausible.

Bill McKibben, an environmentalist scholar, makes the interesting point in *Enough* (2003) that even current environmentalism has added to this cultural zeitgeist: "The movement to value everything else on Earth has often talked carelessly about people, spreading the idea that we are a grim and uncontrollable race, a cancer cell metastasizing unchecked across the defenseless fabric of nature" (112). Certainly, if we have doomed the Earth to suffer (for instance) a runaway greenhouse effect, then it might be better to be living in virtual space than in real space. And there is undeniably an undercurrent of discomfort with bodies seen in many Egan stories, with their lack of physical character descriptions and several rather disastrous and unpleasant depictions of embodied sex. This overall culture of body loathing has consequences. As our media-/image-saturated culture presents versions of beauty that are almost universally digitally enhanced beyond possible physical achievement, many women and men are driven into the realms of anorexia, bulimia, OCD exercise routines, and other intensely unhealthy behaviors. Given that it is not yet possible to abandon our bodies and enter virtual realms where we can all look arbitrarily beautiful, there is still a lot of harm being done here and now by these attitudes.

As a side note, Egan tends to be fairly conservative in describing how characters will present themselves when their image is entirely malleable. He assumes that most people will choose to retain a more-or-less human template. Neal Stephenson is another author who creates digitally mediated characters, particularly in *Snow Crash* (1992). In that novel Stephenson posits a Second Life–style virtual reality. People's avatars (digital images that other inhabitants of the VR scape see) are imbued with all sorts of class and status markers. The hero of the story, Hiro Protagonist, has high status because of his computer skills. His avatar is a detailed and lifelike rendering of himself. Poorer and less creative individuals buy off-the-shelf avatars in the images of popular celebrities. The richer you are, the more computer time you can buy, so that poorer inhabitants use low-resolution avatars that have a level of time-lag in updating their expressions or movements based on the user's inputs. Other users aim for the shock value of challenging middle-American values by having an avatar shaped, for example, like a giant penis. Even if we grant a future in which computer resources are effectively unlimited, such that one's digital presentation would no longer be a class indicator, it is hard to believe that there would not be the equivalent of the giant-penis guys and celebrity-derivative folks running around. But they do not feature in Egan's fiction.

Returning to critiques of the posthuman project, Mary Midgley's *Science as Salvation: A Modern Myth and its Meaning* (1992) is suspicious of the dangled promise of immortality. While she looks primarily at the rhetoric of scientists in the popular press, there is no doubt that science fiction in general, and Egan's work in particular, reinforces these messages. One of Midgley's points is: "In the first place, of course, there is here a power fantasy. 'We' are going to become supreme in the universe" (154). Also: "I have already mentioned two crude motives for this kind of prophecy—the fear of death and the lust for power" (163). When it comes to power struggles, Egan has a surprising spin on this. He does not see humanity triumphing over other sentient species in the universe; in the Amalgam future many alien species coexist harmoniously because there are enough resources for everyone to be largely content—there is no inherent need for conflict. However, he does see humanity taking control of its fate in the universe through our strides in *understanding* the universe. Egan usually casts this in terms of preventing our extermination from existential threats: in *Diaspora*, humanity is almost wiped out by an unpredicted celestial event, and the posthumans start exploring to find out how to protect themselves from a galaxy-wide equivalent. In *Incandescence*, the aliens have to prevent their world from spiralling into a black hole. While there is no doubt that this resonates with historical rhetoric demanding that nature be "subjugated" to human control and will, it can also be seen as an attempt to understand nature such that we can modify both it and ourselves to exist harmoniously.

Midgley also describes one consequence of drawing a sharp divide between mind and matter, where all of nature is simply matter and cannot have any "mysterious intrinsic properties" (48). In this conception, animals are objectified and treated as mere automata. However, Egan has almost exactly the opposite attitude. On those rare occasions when he mentions animals in his stories, he treats them with the same respect that he does sentient beings (and he is himself vegetarian). His early story "The Demon's Passage" is clearly against animal experimentation, and in works such as *Incandescence* and "Crystal Nights" he argues strongly against experimenting on even simulations of conscious beings. Fundamentally, Egan sees humanity, even when transformed into digital posthumanity, as fully integrated into the natural world, never standing aloof from it. This may also relate to his personal atheism; when there is no afterlife to attend to, one has little choice but to be fully part of the material universe.

In another section, Midgley argues that the posthumanist disembodied future is significantly different from other literary utopias. Whereas utopian fictions such as More's sui generis *Utopia* or Bellamy's *Looking Backward* were written to point out the flaws in their author's societies, these transhumanist futures sidestep most of those problems altogether. "They are not interested in making our existing human life better, nor in understanding it, nor even in simply making it work, but in getting away from it" (162). This can be seen in Egan's rough future history where there's a distinct gap between the world of "Yeyuka" or *Permutation City* (where life-extending or brain-uploading technology is available only to the wealthy) and that of *Diaspora* (where it is ubiquitous). After that point, Egan throws out many sources of current political problems: Starvation? Not an issue. Global warming? We'll leave a much smaller footprint on the planets. Class differences? Plenty of computing resources for all. Territorial squabbles? Here, have a planet! Room enough for everyone. Religious differences? Won't be an issue when everyone can have their own place to live as they see fit. The word "optimism" hardly seems adequate.

Another interesting omission from Egan's far-future stories is any kind of malevolent software or other accidental interruption of service. In *Mind Children*,

Hans Moravec devotes an entire chapter to the role of malware (computer viruses and other bugs) in a digital ecosystem. He argues that these things will never be entirely eliminated; while people may possibly leave off intentional hacking (unlikely), some bugs are simply likely to evolve in extremely complex systems. He takes the viewpoint that this is a good thing, as it will keep people on their toes and spur beneficial evolution—"fruitful chaos," he cheerfully terms it. One suspects that our digital descendants would not take so light a view. However, Egan's characters never even mention the possibility. He points out: "In the very long term—the *Schild's Ladder* or *Diaspora* time frame—when we've completely rebuilt all the hardware and software infrastructure many times over, and when their robustness and security are life-and-death matters for most of the population most of the time, I'm quite sure there'll be no systemic freezes and crashes, or low-level viruses" (Burnham interview). However, he then goes on to note that the character of Yatima, whose birth is detailed in the first chapter of *Diaspora*, titled "Orphanogenesis," could be considered a bug—certainly, its existence was not planned.

Looking back at the philosophical criticism, some of the protests have the same feel and moral grounding as complaints about space exploration: How can we reach for the stars when we cannot even solve our problems here at home? That argument has played out many times over the last several decades; in the end society spends money on domestic concerns as well as blue-sky projects such as the International Space Station or the Large Hadron Collider. There is a feeling that we will never completely solve problems such as poverty, and we should not make that a precondition of funding space and science research. Also, there is the sense that history and scientific progress will move forward regardless of those who may stand in the road and yell "Stop!"—rarely have those impulses succeeded in halting the overall momentum of discovery for more than decades or centuries at specific times in specific places. As much as critics pontificate and transhumanists put out newsletters and science fiction authors spin tales, reality will be the ultimate arbiter. If enough people with enough resources decide that a posthuman world of incorruptible information is the direction of the future, very few cultural institutions would have the power to prevent them.

CHAPTER 4

SCIENTIFIC ANALYSIS

Science is central to Greg Egan's approach to literature. The fact that humanity is able to comprehend the fundamental nature of the universe is a source of endless wonder, something his stories constantly seek to illuminate. When reflecting on his writing career, he says:

> If I'm pleased with one general achievement, it's to have contributed something to the very small subset of literature that engages in a meaningful way with the full context of human existence. The fact that we are part of a physical universe whose laws can be discovered through reason and observation is the most profound and powerful insight in our history, but most literature—including a large proportion of SF—either ignores it or trivialises it. I'm not interested in fiction that invites the reader to become slack-jawed with "wonder" at the size of the universe or the time scale of cosmology or the strangeness of quantum mechanics, or that treats the now-long-obvious fact that there is no God and we have no pre-existing purpose as some kind of belittling revelation of our insignificance and

impermanence. Literature that truly engages with reality isn't shocked by things we've known for centuries; rather, it delights in the fact that we've managed to learn so much about the universe and it revels in the details. (Burnham interview)

Egan's stories feature science and scientists who strive in the most intellectual way possible, wrestling with mathematics and experimental physics to extend their understanding of the universe. Kim Stanley Robinson, another hard SF writer featured in *The Hard SF Renaissance*, says:

> Science fiction is rarely about scientists doing real science, in its slowness, its vagueness, the sort of tedious quality of getting out there and digging amongst the rocks and then trying to convince people that what you're seeing justifies the conclusions you're making. The whole process of science is wildly under-represented in science fiction because it's not easy to write about. There are many facets of science that are almost exactly opposite of dramatic narrative. It's slow, tedious, inconclusive, it's hard to tell good guys from bad guys—it's everything that a normal hour of Star Trek is not. (Hartwell and Cramer 2002, 117)

This is not unique to physicists; it is much easier to write about the adventures of an Indiana Jones–type archaeologist than about the dirty, dusty, boring, grant-writing work of real-world archaeology. However, in a genre that identifies so strongly with the scientific fields, it is surprising that so few authors have tackled the joys of even the "hard" parts of science head on.

Given his success in bringing the passion of science to readers through fiction, it is interesting that Egan's forays into science popularization have been less successful—woeful failures may not be overstating the case. In four issues of the Australian SF magazine *Eidolon* in the late 1990s, Egan was given a science column. He wrote a series that, with the help of plentiful diagrams and equations, moved the reader from basic geometry through descriptions of space-time under both special and general relativity and on to quantum mechanics. Dense doesn't begin to describe it, and the columns did not go over particularly well with readers. The articles were followed by letters to the editor, such as:

> Maybe it's just me, but I thought the Greg Egan article was a bit too heavy. I'm fascinated by relativity and its implications, but all those pages of equations lost me. I'd be surprised if I was alone in this—or even a minority. (Rick Kennett, *Eidolon* 28, 128)

and

> . . . but if I want to read something like this I'll buy a physics textbook. (John Bleckley, *Eidolon* 28, 131)

Even as the editors defended the articles, they ended up recommending some skimming:

> Have you tried reading *around* the proofs? (Hey, I know *I* trust Greg's math!) The extraordinary insights into the implications of the geometry of space-time are worth a little brain-bending. (*Eidolon* 28, 128)

Egan is unapologetic about his demands on the reader. Kathryn Cramer wrote: "Before science can be incorporated into hard SF, it must be stripped of its mathematical bones, so that—no matter how accurate the text—science is used as mythology" (James and Mendlesohn 188). When Egan wrote *Incandescence* and the Orthogonal books, he skipped that step and left the mathematical anatomy intact. More than any author since Hal Clement (who published science notes alongside his famous novel *Mission of Gravity* as it was being serialized in John W. Campbell's *Astounding* in 1954), Egan wants his readers to grasp, learn, and come to understand the science behind his stories. In a rare response to a negative review, Adam Roberts's 2008 review of *Incandescence*, Egan writes:

> A few reviewers complained that they had trouble keeping straight the physical meanings of the Splinterites' directions. This leaves me wondering if they've really never encountered a book before that benefits from being read with a pad of paper and a pen beside it, or whether they're just so hung up on the idea that only non-fiction should be accompanied by note-taking and diagram-scribbling that it never even occurred to them to do this. I realise that some people do much of their reading with one hand on a strap in a crowded bus or train carriage, but books simply don't come with a guarantee that they can be properly enjoyed under such conditions. ("Anatomy of a Hatchet Job")

Only a few readers are willing to put that level of work into reading a novel. For them, Egan is perhaps the most rewardingly challenging author publishing today. However, the stories have plenty to offer even those readers who are less scientifically dedicated. Readers and critics who are less inclined to space-time diagrams are still impressed by his work. Egan is a respectable craftsman at the sentence level, and the sense of wonder is accessible even to those who don't grasp all the details of the mathematics. The resonances between science and society that he illuminates are meaningful to a broad swath of readers.

This chapter cannot hope to explain all the nuances of all the science behind Egan's dozen novels and sixty-plus short stories. Instead, it will give an overview of the quantum mechanics and "subjective cosmology" of *Quarantine*, *Permutation City* and *Distress*; the mathematical approach to cosmology and relativity seen in *Diaspora*, *Schild's Ladder*, and *Incandescence*; and the alternate physics described in the Orthogonal trilogy, focusing on *Clockwork Rocket* and *Eternal Flame* (the concluding novel *The Arrows of Time* had, at the time of writing, only just been published and therefore is not included in the detailed analysis here). *Teranesia* and *Zendegi* are not considered in detail—they are both near-future works in which scientific breakthroughs are less significant than the character-based stories at their hearts.

On the web pages related to the Orthogonal universe, Egan posts a large, boxed-out warning: "Many of the pages linked below contain 'conceptual' spoilers: although they make no reference to the plot of *Orthogonal*, they cover scientific matters that are only revealed gradually in the novel." Needless to say, this chapter will also involve a lot of conceptual spoilers. Perhaps only science fiction needs this kind of warning. While most people think of a "spoiler" as something that gives away the ending of a book—perhaps by revealing the murderer in a murder mystery—the joys of reading Egan's fiction are not primarily found in the plot. Instead, they are found in the gradual revealing and deepening understanding of the world, either our own universe and its potential or an alternate cosmology.

Egan's stories are often driven by the "conceptual breakthrough," as the *SF Encyclopedia* would have it, where the climax of the novel occurs when the characters make a leap in understanding something fundamental about their world. This structure has a long history in science fiction. For instance, in Robert Heinlein's "Universe" (1941), the characters live in an enclosed space, and they believe that the space they inhabit encompasses the entire universe, that there is nothing outside their walls. Both they and the reader slowly come to understand that they are living on board a generation starship, a slower-than-light ship meant to support multiple generations of people while they make the centuries-long journey to another solar system. The characters in "Universe" have been in the ship so long that they have forgotten its purpose, and the rediscovery is a revelation for them and a twist ending for the reader. The aliens in Egan's *Incandescence* make a very similar journey, although one based on more abstruse physics. Thus, while it is no spoiler to say that a particular murder mystery is set in a small town in England, it could be a spoiler to reveal that the Splinter in *Incandescence* is orbiting a black hole. This is characteristic of the puzzle-solving nature of many SF stories.

For more in-depth information on the science of Egan's science fiction, there are several excellent resources for the interested reader. Egan's own website has a significant amount of extra information about the physics involved in his stories. There he provides equations, diagrams, and Java applets that illustrate some of the concepts in animated form. The animations are particularly helpful—a classic case of a picture (or short animation) being worth a thousand words—while several of the applets are interactive, so the reader can, for instance, play different iterations of a game of quantum soccer as described in the story "Border Guards."

The other critical resource for the intensely interested reader is the epic tome *Gravitation* by superstar physicists Charles Misner, Kip Thorne, and John Wheeler. Describing the book in a short piece for the website *Suvudu*, Egan writes:

> In the 1980s I tried a couple of times to teach myself general relativity, but I chose the wrong books and found myself baffled and dispirited. . . . It was only in 1996 that I finally came across *Gravitation* by Charles Misner, Kip Thorne and John Wheeler. Published in 1973, this 1,279-page masterpiece takes all the time it needs to prepare the reader for the subject, spelling out the beautiful geometric principles that underly [sic] Einstein's conception of gravity. . . . This book gives you the mathematics you need, defined with care, but backs it all the way with physical intuition. I only wish I'd read it twenty years earlier. (Egan "Booked")

For the more general reader, Chad Orzel's books *How to Explain Physics to Your Dog* and *How to Explain Relativity to Your Dog* may provide useful insights into the physics behind *Quarantine*, *Incandescence*, and the Orthogonal universe. They also happen to feature an Egan-style Socratic dialogue as the main structure of explanation, in this case between Professor Orzel and his very smart dog Emmy. Still, it is important to remember that even with an imperfect understanding of the physical and mathematical underpinnings of these stories, there are plenty of other rewards available to the reader.

SUBJECTIVE COSMOLOGY

Perhaps no field of modern physics is as gloriously confounding and confusing to our normal sense of how the world works as quantum mechanics. Because of its impossible-seeming statements (Light is both a particle and a wave! Particles can cross from point A to point B without occupying the space in between!), it seems easy to believe that anything is possible. However, far from being magical or mysterious, quantum mechanics makes predictions that are very specific and have been precisely confirmed by repeated scientific experiments. While those results tell us that a lot of what we know about classical physics is wrong, Egan notes: "There is still no firm consensus as to exactly what should replace the classical view" ("Quantum Mechanics and Quarantine"). We can now describe and predict the behavior of particles on a very small scale, but what it all *means* is still a matter of intense debate.

In *Quarantine*, the fundamental phenomenon driving the book is something called a "wave function." Every individual particle has a wave function, and among other things it describes the probability of finding a particle in a region of space. Remember that at this level we are talking about particles such as electrons or photons up to atoms and molecules, nothing as large as even a (comparatively enormous) speck of dust. Egan reminds us:

> In classical mechanics every object possesses a definite location; we might be ignorant of it, or only know it approximately, but this single, definite location exists nonetheless. In quantum mechanics, a particle such as a photon or an electron will generally exist in a state where it might be found, with various probabilities, anywhere across a range of locations. It's important to understand that this is *not* the same as a lack of precision in our ability to measure things; . . . a photon . . . is *not* simply like a pea that we're told might be under either of two thimbles, but in fact is definitely under just one. ("Quantum Mechanics and Quarantine")

The quantum particle can be demonstrated to exist in multiple locations at once until it is measured:

> The wave function describes a particle whose location is spread out over several centimetres, but when we make a measurement to see where the particle is, we

> find it in *just one place*. What's more, if we check again (very quickly, so as not to give the particle time to move or spread out), we will find it in the same place again. Like a tossed coin that's finally hit the ground head up, or a pea that's been revealed beneath the first thimble from the left, the alternative possibilities that we couldn't rule out until the measurement was made seem to have gone away. For the coin and the pea this doesn't surprise us; they could only ever do one thing at a time. But the whole point of quantum mechanics is that multiple possibilities *must* have co-existed before we made the measurement. ("Quantum Mechanics and Quarantine")

This moment is referred to as the wave-function *collapse*, and it is perhaps one of the most mysterious (although predictable and observable) phenomena in all of physics. What happens when the wave function collapses? How and why does a particle that used to exist in multiple places at once all of a sudden decided to pick one spot and stay there? What is the role of the observer? This is where the magical-sounding "Many Worlds Interpretation" of quantum mechanics comes from: it is the hypothesis that for every wave-function collapse, a separate universe spawns for every possible outcome. If a photon may be at point A or point B, when the wave function collapses there is one universe where it is seen at point A, and another where it is seen at point B. This sounds fantastic and science fictional, but there is nothing known about quantum mechanics or the rest of physics that specifically rules it out as a potential mechanism. It has been the basis of any number of SF stories—for instance Ian McDonald's novel *Planesrunner* (December 2011), the first of a series written for young adults.

Quarantine takes a slightly different approach to the phenomenon. The story looks at the role of the *observer* in causing the wave function to collapse. Our hero, Nick Stavrianos, gains access to technology that allows him to postpone the wave function's collapse (on a macroscopic scale, which would be impossible no matter which interpretation of quantum physics one believes in) as long as he is unobserved by any other people. The premise of the story is that there is something unique about the human brain that causes wave functions to collapse, and that in the rest of the universe uncollapsed waveforms interact with each other to create a richly diverse environment, an environment to which humanity represents a threat. Aliens quarantine the solar system from the rest of the universe, trying to prevent our observations from collapsing their wave functions. As part of a thriller plot, Nick is able to, for instance, try all combinations of a lock at once, only collapsing the wave function in the instance where he is able to open it—as long as he can go unnoticed. Egan is very clear that "*Quarantine* centered on a tongue-in-cheek, science-fictional resolution of that controversy, with a hypothesis that was chosen solely for its technological and existential ramifications, not because I considered it plausible" ("Quantum Mechanics and Quarantine"). On his website he lays out clearly what parts of the scenario are implausible and why he now believes that it would be *impossible*, even if the observer effect turned out to be real.

Permutation City and *Distress* hinge less on the subtleties of quantum physics and more on speculative metaphysics. In *Permutation City*, "Dust Theory" is a hypothesis that imagines that in any amount of material ("dust"), an infinite number of patterns persist. Some of those patterns contain conscious observers, and those observers could experience the world just like we do—in fact, our perception of the universe could be a single iteration (or permutation) of pattern in the dust. This is a bit like imagining that our universe is a simulation on a computer in some other universe, except this posits a conglomeration of material that can simulate every possible universe. Again, Egan does not give this much credence as a "true" description of reality, but his characters dramatize this potential as they digitize themselves, spawn a pocket universe, and load their backups into it. There is no way to test this hypothesis, given the physics we know today, but it has the potential to let the science-fictional imagination soar.

Distress offers a story grounded in the world of science as it is practiced today, set at a scientific conference where the members are trying to make their mathematical and empirical arguments while managing a media circus outside. The plot hinges on some players in that circus, specifically the followers of a fringe cult who have an outlandish take on the problem of observers and the universe that they call anthrocosmology. They imagine a universe that starts as a blank slate of potential structure. When observers run tests and make measurements, physical laws come into being to make the observations consistent across the entire universe, analogous to a quantum mechanical observer collapsing a wave function and finding a particle in position A—now everyone who comes after will agree that the particle is in location A and not B. The anthrocosmologists believe that observers create reality instead of vice versa, and that whoever can come up with a consistent Theory of Everything (a physical theory that explains everything we know about the physics of our universe) will in fact cause the universe to snap into agreement with that theory. They call this person the Alpha, and they believe that they can influence which person will become the Alpha. At the scientific conference at the heart of the novel, there are three researchers who are presenting Theories of Everything, and the anthrocosmologists are working behind the scenes to influence which one ends up being successful. This is a hypothesis so ludicrous that it seems out of keeping with the rest of Egan's fiction, but it drives a story that reflects many of his main themes and does so powerfully.

In a sense, these three books have the least rigorous, most speculative and hand-waving science to be found in Egan's oeuvre. They serve as slightly softer on-ramps for many readers to come to know and enjoy his storytelling. When he was writing these books, Egan was asked: "Why does 'philosophy of consciousness / nature of reality' seem to interest you so much?" He responded: "Take away consciousness and reality and there's not much left" (*Eidolon* 15).

WORKING OUT OUR UNIVERSE

Egan's approach to blending "real world" physics and speculative physics in *Diaspora* and *Schild's Ladder* can be seen in this after-the-story glossary entry from *Diaspora*:

> **Kozuch Theory.** A provisional unified theory of physics developed in the mid-twenty-first century. Kozuch Theory describes the universe as a ten-dimensional fiber bundle; its size in six dimensions is sub-microscopic, so only the familiar four dimensions of space-time are immediately apparent. Particles such as electrons are actually the mouths of very narrow wormholes, an idea first suggested by the twentieth-century physicist John Wheeler. Renata Kozuch developed a model in which the properties of different particles are due to the different ways wormhole mouths can be connected in the six extra dimensions. (*Diaspora* 283)

This is essentially a piece of flash fiction, expanding a speculative idea from real-world scientist John Wheeler into a potential future theory. Egan does the same thing with the very short story "Only Connect," which appeared in the prestigious scientific journal *Nature* and which lays out the (invented) Quantum Graph Theory that is fundamental to *Schild's Ladder*. In that short piece Egan traces a strand of thought from Michael Faraday (mid-nineteenth century) to Roger Penrose (born 1931 and still active) to John Baez (mathematical physicist and contemporary of Egan's) to the entirely fictional Javanese scientist Kusnanto Sarumpaet operating in the 2030s.

It should be noted that this scientific approach is quite different from science fiction's more common engineering stories. When one thinks of "hard SF," one sometimes thinks of stories from the pages of *Analog* magazine. *Analog* is the continuation of John W. Campbell's *Astounding* magazine, and over the past three decades it has become known for publishing a very specific sort of physics-/engineering-based puzzle-solving story. The characters are presented with a scenario, be it a broken spaceship, failing spacesuit, incomprehensible alien, and so on, and must apply some sort of hard science or engineering principle in order to resolve the situation. Egan never gained much traction at *Analog*, instead becoming a regular in the pages of *Interzone* and *Asimov's*. While *Analog* stories often feature speculative science and engineering marvels, they tend to do so in a relatively limited way. Instead of reaching for knowledge about the fundamental underpinnings of the universe, they look for applications of new knowledge to specific problems. Some of Egan's stories do that as well (one need look no further than "Cocoon" for social implications and "Into Darkness" for a pure puzzle-solving story), but at their core they tend to reach for those boundaries where science shades into philosophy instead of the areas where science shades into engineering.

In *Incandescence*, the aliens inhabiting the Splinter start off rather more working-class than elite scientific minds. During normal times, there are only a few things that need to get done to ensure that the Splinter functions as an ecosystem and as a community. Individuals get satisfaction from joining teams and pitching in to make sure the work gets done. Occasionally, people change work teams or roles, and there's space in the system to allow that to happen. Roi has been part of a farming team before she meets Zak, an eccentric who has obviously been doing something very different. As she learns more about what he is doing, she decides to leave her team and join him. As they realize just how precarious their world's existence is, they begin to recruit others, forming their own team.

What the aliens do over the course of their story is to discover almost everything known about general relativity and the space-time structure of the universe without using either astronomy or computers. Showing how this could be done is a remarkable achievement, a thought experiment on a grand fictional scale. In our history almost everything we understand about the universe was originally motivated by astronomy, and it is almost impossible to separate the idea of "science" from that of "computers" in popular consciousness.

In our history of science, we started with astronomy and small-scale experiments with normal-scaled objects and (after a few thousand years) arrived at the Newtonian understanding of the universe. In the nineteenth century, Newtonian physics and the field of electromagnetism both seemed to make perfect sense, with Newton's Three Laws and the four formulae describing electromagnetism now known as Maxwell's equations. However, a problem arose when the speed of light predicted by Maxwell's equations did not obey Newtonian physics.

Imagine you are driving a car and you throw a ball out the window ahead of you. You see it move ahead of you at the speed you threw it. An observer standing off to the side sees the ball moving at the speed of the car plus the speed at which you threw it. However, when you are in a car and you turn the headlights on, you see the light move away from you at the speed of light, and the person on the side of the road *also* sees the light moving at the speed of light—every observer sees light moving at the same speed, no matter their perspective. This is the heart of all the weirdness that makes up relativity. Earlier models were expanded and contorted to try to accommodate these contradictions but in the end Einstein's theory of relativity was the simplest and most accurate, no matter how counterintuitive. Since the formulation of the theory of relativity, many of the most dramatic proofs of its existence have come from astronomical observations—the orbit of Mercury, Doppler-shifting of light, gravitational lensing, and the like. Evidence for time dilation includes observations of muons that arrive at ground-level detectors, created by high-energy particle collisions with cosmic rays high in the atmosphere. *Incandescence* compresses at least three hundred years of human scientific progress into a single generation, and it leaves out pretty much all nonrelevant branches of science: no electromagnetism, chemistry, electrical engineering, quantum mechanics, and so on. But through it, Egan shows how the same fundamental understanding of a relativistic universe can be developed by watching rocks move, without bringing light into the picture at all.

Just as humanity started out with an intuitive understanding that the Earth is fixed in space and the Sun moves around it, at the very beginning of the story Zak and Roi know that they inhabit a volume of rock (the Splinter) that is bounded, and that outside of their domain is a "wind" (the "Incandescence" of the title) that provides nutrients but is harmful if experienced directly without walls of rock to protect them. They have no sense of orbiting some other body (the black hole called the Hub) and never observe that body directly.

Probably the single most important thing needed in order to visualize the alien's situation is orbital dynamics. The orbital dynamics of a Newtonian universe are quite different from those in a general relativity universe, and orbits near a black hole exaggerate those differences to the point that they are easily observable within short periods. The Splinter completes one orbit around the Hub in only a few minutes—we take a year to complete the same circuit around the Sun. The astronauts on the International Space Station (ISS) could conduct all the same observations that the Splinterites do—ISS's orbit around the Earth only takes ninety minutes. However, the Earth is so small compared to a black hole that they would need much more sensitive instruments to observe the effects that the aliens can see plainly. It should be noted that the way things move in free space is so counterintuitive (even without taking relativity into account) that astronauts have trouble maneuvering on orbit until they have received extensive, specific training. The Gemini 4 mission in 1965 had a rendezvous attempt (with the upper stage of its launch rocket) tacked on to the mission goals at the last minute, so the astronauts had no time to train. The attempt was extremely frustrating and ultimately unsuccessful. The rendezvous maneuver was finally successful during Gemini 6A's mission a few months later, once the astronauts had had time to understand and train with the applicable physics.

The problem is that an orbit is not like a racetrack where you can complete a lap in either one minute (faster) or two minutes (slower). For each unique orbit around the Earth, there is only one speed at which you can complete a single circuit. The International Space Station makes a full circuit around the Earth once every ninety minutes. If it needed to circle the Earth faster it could not simply "speed up." Instead, it would need to move to a lower orbit, which has a smaller circle and can be completed more quickly. Likewise, to "slow down" it would need to rise up to a larger orbit that would take more time to complete. The upshot of all this is that if you simply thrust forward to try to reach something ahead of you, you end up changing your orbit and may miss your target altogether. That was the problem that the Gemini 4 astronauts ran into: when they tried to move toward their rendezvous target, they ended up passing below it instead. It takes a lot of training to counteract your intuition about relative motion such that when you want to move toward something, you remember to thrust down instead.

Also remember that we are only aware of experiencing force when we bump up against something that is not moving the same way we are. We experience weight and gravity because gravity pulls us against the surface of the Earth, which stops us from going any farther. We experience the balance between the downward pull of gravity and the resistance to motion of the Earth's surface as weight. Astronauts on the ISS are also under the influence of the Earth's gravitational field, but they do not feel it (instead experiencing weightlessness) because they and the space station are all moving together—there is nothing stopping them from moving with their appropriate acceleration.

In the Splinter then, there is a place at the center of the asteroid called the Null Chamber where all the forces balance out and everything is moving together. Specifically, there is the Null Line, which is the arc of the Splinter's orbital path. It is large enough compared to the asteroid that it seems to be a straight line. People on that line feel weightless, and stones placed there don't move. However, when people move away from the Null Line, they are pressed against the walls of the asteroid to a greater or lesser degree depending on their position within the asteroid. Stones displaced from the line will move with their own orbital dynamics unless stopped by a wall. Almost everything that Zak and Roi's team discover about their universe comes from observing the behavior of those rocks floating in that chamber. All the technology they need for their experiments is based on rocks, tubes, and springs.

As the Splinterites start the story, all Zak has is a map that shows that as you leave the Null Chamber by moving above or below the orbital plane, your perceived weight increases and you feel yourself pulled back toward the chamber; but if you leave the chamber going toward or away from the Hub, your weight increases more quickly, and you feel yourself pulled away from the chamber instead. According to the map, the ratio of these increases in weight is 3:1. One of the most important things in the novel (philosophically speaking) happens early on: Zak and Roi go to measure these increases for themselves, instead of relying on an ancient scroll of unknown provenance, and they discover that the ratios are not 3:1. They are actually closer to 2.25:1. This is monumental, on the same scale as human science shaking off the notion, dictated by ancient aesthetics instead of observations, that planetary orbits (models that allow us to predict where visible planets such as Jupiter and Venus will appear in the sky) must be circular—in fact, we now know that they are elliptical. The 3:1 ratio would be correct in a purely Newtonian system, and may have been roughly true in the asteroid's past, when it may have been farther away from the Hub. But they are so near to the black hole at the center of their system, with its very steep gravitational gradient, that the ratios they measure are quite different. Over the course of the story Zak and Roi learn about their orbital motion, infer the existence of the Hub, develop the language of vectors and algebra, discover Kepler's laws (describing planetary orbits), set up the equivalent of a Foucault's pendulum, and parse out most of the rules of general relativity. They discover the "critical speed" by observing that if an object travels faster than a critical speed, the distance traveled would have to be an imaginary number in order to satisfy the equations. Since that is impossible, it is impossible for an object to travel faster than the critical speed—the speed of light. The aliens calculate the speed of light without ever measuring it and without connecting it to light in any way, a remarkable feat of reasoning about the universe and a stunningly elegant result.

It is only toward the end of the book that the Splinterites have a brief opportunity to conduct astronomical observations. When Roi goes out to look at the stars, she sees them not as steady points of white light but as objects whose color is constantly shifting. But the stars display a periodic motion across the sky, which relates to the Splinter's orbital motion. Their changing color is caused by the Doppler-shifting of the light as it follows different paths through the warped region of space-time surrounding the black hole. At this point they notice an object that is not following the same fixed patterns—the Wanderer. This is a large body that, by approaching too near to the Splinter, has knocked their orbit out of its previous orbital plane. As both the Splinter and the Wanderer spiral in toward the Hub, they are starting to interfere with each other, and the Wanderer is another existential threat to the Splinter: if the Splinter spirals in past the event horizon, it will be destroyed by the black hole, but if it simply stabilizes its orbit, it might collide with the much larger Wanderer.

Zak, Roi, and their growing research team are able to make use of gravitational lensing (where a strong gravitational field, like that of a black hole, bends light around itself) to measure the extent to which the Wanderer has its own space-time geometry independent of the Hub's. It is only when they need to precisely measure this subtle effect that they develop basic telescopes. In our world we made astronomical observations from the beginning, recording the different periodic motions of the objects in the sky long before we developed any formal understanding of physics. Our descriptions of space-time lagged behind the development of telescopes by about four hundred years.

For the Splinterites, the combination of the gravitational field of the Wanderer and the space-time curvature of the Hub makes it impossible to calculate or simulate how small nudges to the Splinter will affect its orbit. Even in Newtonian space the three-body problem cannot be solved algebraically. Instead, it must be calculated by taking small segments of time and computing how all the forces act on all the bodies from one time step to the next. But that brute-force approach will not work for the extreme space-time curvature caused by the Hub, due to the nonlinear nature of the equations associated with general relativity, at least not on any feasible time scale. The computations would simply take too long to generate a useful answer. For protection from whatever fate (or stellar physics) has in store for the Wanderer, the Splinterites need to lock themselves into an orbit that places them on the opposite side of the Hub from the Wanderer—sharing an orbit but 180 degrees apart. That way, the Wanderer will never get close enough to them to destabilize their orbit. It is difficult, especially since the Wanderer is not in a perfectly circular orbit, but with their understanding of the space-time geometry and orbits involved, they are able to find the safest possible course. And when the Wanderer eventually explodes, they are largely shielded by the Hub. In this way, using math, physics, and some rocks, they are able to save themselves from annihilation.

In order to make this all work, the aliens have to be both incredibly good at physics and incredibly lucky. There are no delays caused by libraries being burned; by spending centuries going down blind alleys of incorrect physics models; by the mathematics not keeping up with the physics or vice versa; by key scientists dying of plague or hunger; by being denied grants or resource allocations to conduct the necessary experiments. In addition, the Wanderer knocks their orbit out of the plane of the Incandescence long enough for them to conduct some necessary astronomy instead of destroying them instantly or sending them hurtling toward the Hub. Still, by the end of the story Egan has succeeded in his stated goal: "*Incandescence* grew out of the notion that the theory of general relativity—widely regarded as one of the pinnacles of human intellectual achievement—could be discovered by a pre-industrial civilisation with no steam engines, no electric lights, no radio transmitters, and absolutely no tradition of astronomy" ("Big Idea," *Whatever*, July 22, 2008).

Jonathan McCalmont had an interesting insight in his review of *Incandescence*:

> The bulk of the book is devoted to these twin projects and they perfectly reflect each other; Roi has no scientific materials and is forced to work out everything from first principles while Rakesh can draw upon all of human knowledge and construct scientific measuring devices at will but, despite the radical differences between the two groups in terms of access to resources, both use the same mode of scientific thought; coming up with hypotheses, running tests and then working out the meaning of the data. This is an interesting concept for a novel. (McCalmont)

One may argue over whether that is a desirable or enjoyable goal for a science fiction novel, and the answer will vary from reader to reader (many critics excoriated the book for being dull). But in showing an alternate route to some of the most fundamental understandings of the universe, Egan reiterates to the reader the illuminating insight that the universe is *discoverable* and *understandable*—not just to the high priests of science in shiny labs full of computers and beam splitters, but to anyone who can bang rocks together and has enough time and patience to observe what the universe has to show us.

ALTERNATE PHYSICS

Having explored the laws of physics as we find them in our universe, in the Orthogonal trilogy Egan conducts an elaborate thought experiment with a universe based on a single change to the laws of physics as we know them. The world-building structure is similar to that of an alternate history, where a single change in our history causes any number of changes large and small to propagate forward. Since an alternate history story is most effective when the reader understands what change has been made, common points of divergence include having the Germans win WWII or having the Confederacy win the U.S. Civil War. Changes in even slightly less famous historical events, such as having the USS Maine fail to explode in Havana harbor, run the risk that the reader will not realize what, if anything, is different. If the story and characters are compelling, this may be no obstacle to enjoyment. On the other hand, it can lead to immense confusion.

Egan runs this same risk with the alternate cosmology of the Orthogonal trilogy, with the added challenge of overcoming general scientific illiteracy. The audience for whom the divergence point in his physics will be obvious is relatively small. Even with the help of the explanatory material on his website (running more than eighty thousand words of text and more than one hundred illustrations, all uploaded well in advance of the books' release) for those readers more familiar with Newton's version of physics than Einstein's it can still be hard to follow. The fundamental difference between our universe and Orthogonal comes down to geometry (as is appropriate, considering that Egan is first and foremost a mathematician; here, he is working with the tool set of a mathematical physicist). He draws a distinction between our universe, which he labels Lorentzian, and the Orthogonal universe, which he labels Riemannian. Hendrik Antoon Lorentz (1853–1928) formalized the mathematics that allowed Einstein to describe relativity. Most important for our purposes, the math that describes our universe has four dimensions: three in space and one in time, and the geometry of the time dimension is very different from the space dimensions. As Egan explains in "Plus, Minus: A Gentle Introduction to the Physics of Orthogonal":

> Nobody is surprised that different paths through space between the same two points can have different lengths. If I drive by the most direct route from Perth to Sydney, while you take a detour to Darwin along the way, it's hardly shocking to suggest that our odometers will show us having travelled different distances. We now understand that detours in space-time can have an analogous effect on the passage of time. If you "travel" from New Year's Eve in 2050 to New Year's Eve in 2060 by staying on the Earth, whereas I, though joining you on both occasions, spend the intervening period travelling to Alpha Centauri and back, I will have aged about six years, compared to your ten.

When only spatial dimensions are involved, we can use Pythagoras's Theorem, where the squares of two sides of a right triangle add up to the square of the hypotenuse. However, if one of the sides of the triangle is in time instead of distance, the equivalent formula involves a difference instead of a sum, such that a person traveling a longer path experiences less time passing than a person remaining stationary.

In contrast, for the Orthogonal books Egan proposes a Riemannian universe. Georg Friedrich Bernhard Riemann (1826–1866) was a mathematician who generalized forms of geometry such that they described curved surfaces as well as the flat ones traditional to Euclidian geometry. Egan proposes extending his geometry into four dimensions and treating all the dimensions in the same way, such that triangles with time as one side will still obey Pythagoras's Theorem. While this seems to be a more intuitively comfortable system, it produces some impressively non-intuitive results.

Perhaps the first surprise is that it removes the light-speed limit from the Orthogonal universe. In our Lorentzian universe, if you try to travel five light years in four years, the math works out such that you will arrive after the square root of negative nine years, an imaginary amount of time (remember that negative numbers don't have real square roots). To avoid traveling negative amounts of time, the fastest you can travel five light years is five years, no matter what. This puts a finite cap on the velocity with which anything in the universe can travel. In the Orthogonal universe however, if you try to travel five light years in four years (as clocked by a stationary observer) you will make the journey in 6.4 years (as experienced by the traveler), removing the cap on maximum velocity.

One easily observable consequence of this is that different colors of light have different speeds in the Orthogonal universe. In our universe, different *colors* of light have different *wavelengths* (red light has a longer wavelength than blue light) but all light travels at the same speed, the speed of light. And it might be said that in the Orthogonal universe, all light has a constant behavior in space-time. However, because of the Riemannian geometry (again, there are good diagrams to illustrate this point on Egan's website), light that appears to have a longer wavelength, such as red light, will be traveling more slowly with respect to an observer than light with a shorter wavelength. This is shown in the novel through the prismatic star trails that make up the night sky on Yalda's planet. Where we look up and see a single point of light in the night sky representing a star (looking bluish or reddish depending on the star's age and composition), when Yalda looks up at the sky: "She lifted her rear gaze to watch the stars come out. The trails of light that emerged were like multicolored worms struggling across the deepening blackness—though they appeared to be struggling in vain, swept across the sky in a slow whirl but coming no closer to their destinations" (*Clockwork Rocket* 11). If you imagine a star a moderate distance away, say ten or twenty light years, it has some relative motion compared to an observer on Yalda's planet. It emits light at a certain point, and the blue light arrives first, then the red light arrives. At another point later on, the same thing happens. So Yalda sees blue light coming from its most recent position, and red light coming from its older position, and all the colors in between spread across an arc of sky.

None of that, however, is the oddest part of the world building. The really counterintuitive part may be best represented by the fact that plants open up to emit light at night and close up during the day. What could account for this? We need to examine energy in terms of the Riemannian geometry. In our universe, a stationary object has a certain amount of rest mass energy (represented by the famous $E=mc^2$). When it starts moving, it gains a certain amount of kinetic energy, raising the total energy of the system. However, in the Orthogonal universe a moving object has *less* energy because of the way the vectors add up in space and time.

This does not change the behavior of day-to-day objects, since the only time the energy versus rest-mass comparison becomes apparent is at the level of nuclear reactions or the behavior of light. Playing a game of baseball would not be noticeably different under these rules. However, the implication of kinetic energy subtracting from the energy of the system means that something with zero rest mass would never be able to move, since the total energy of the system would then be negative. In our universe photons have zero rest mass but in the Orthogonal universe they must have a finite rest mass. So reactions that create light in the Orthogonal universe end up with more kinetic energy than they had at the beginning (thus, counterintuitively, conserving the energy of the system). This energy can manifest as motion or heat, or it can be stored as chemical energy. Thus when the flowers are shining, they are creating chemical energy to store. Finding stable arrangements of matter in these circumstances would be delicate and rare, which the story reflects by showing chemistry to be a dangerous occupation with a high casualty rate. The question of the stability of matter is central to the second book in the trilogy. It may be a little hard to suspend disbelief and accept that a universe with such physical laws could support any life at all, but without that conceit there could be no story.

This only scratches the surface of the interesting implications for physics caused by using Riemannian geometry and by forcing time to play by space-like rules. Egan has propagated the changes through to the fields of electromagnetism, thermodynamics, general relativity, and quantum mechanics, all of which change dramatically under the new rules. Within the pages of the novel he limits himself to working out the physics through dialog between characters, with diagrams included as the characters discuss them. The diagrams are particularly important; even today, perhaps the most important tool that a scientist or engineer possesses is a chalkboard or whiteboard on which to sketch and erase, ensuring that all participants in a conversation are talking about the same thing. Describing the mathematics of the Riemannian universe using only day-to-day language is tricky at best; for those with mathematical training it comes as almost a relief to read either the appendices or the information on Egan's website, where he lays out all the necessary equations. There is a reason that mathematics has developed a specialized language that allows huge amounts of information to be conveyed in a minimum of space. Having to refer to second and third rates of change instead of being able to refer to derivatives (familiar to those who have learned calculus) can make it even harder to follow the developments of the ideas. However, it is an understandable attempt to keep the speculative aspects of the story as broadly accessible as possible. For the more technically minded reader, there is enough supplementary material on Egan's website to fill a PhD-level dissertation on the subject—if any school were willing to grant a doctorate based on the physics of an imaginary universe.

PROCESS OF SCIENCE, SCIENCE IN CULTURE

While Egan often dramatizes the process of science, it is something that he does to greater and lesser extents in different books and stories. If one compares *Distress* (1995) and *Teranesia* (1999), *Distress* clearly has more to say about how science happens in society than *Teranesia*. In the latter, protagonist Prabir Suresh joins a biology field researcher in the Indonesian islands, but he does so almost solely in the hopes of keeping tabs on his sister, who has joined a better-funded and better-organized expedition with the same goals. In his time in the islands Prabir learns all the science needed to drive the resolution of the plot, but the main thrust of the narrative is his relationship with his sister and with his past. In *Distress*, the reporter Andrew Worth is attending a scientific convention, the Einstein Centenary conference, on a genetically engineered island. He is there to report for a feature on Violet Mosala, a physicist with a theory that appears to be the leading contender to be accepted as the Theory of Everything. There are other contenders, and the different factions inevitably engage in political maneuvring. There are press conferences, paper sessions, and back-room arguments. This has much more in common with science as it is practiced day to day and year on year in the world, although of course, most physics conferences are not broken up by terrorists. *Zendegi*, another near-future book, while it does not focus so much on pure science, is sensitive to the political concerns that arise whenever fraught issues such as consciousness and souls are under discussion. Different computer companies looking to develop better AI for their nonplayer characters come under attack from various angles: from the media, from religious sectors, and from fringe groups.

In the far future of *Incandescence*, the research and eventual engineering takes place in what seems like a societal vacuum. As the aliens' biology awakens their potential for curiosity and ingenuity in response to a perceived crisis, they achieve consensus on almost everything that needs to be done. There are occasional disagreements, but they are all easily resolved by calculation and proof. When their first engineering attempt goes badly wrong (one of the tunnels dug through the rock in order to modify their orbit causes part of the Splinter to fissure, in turn causing disruption and scores of deaths), there is no movement to stop what they are doing and reconsider. Compare that to the social and media reactions to even such a relatively small-scale catastrophe as Three Mile Island (with zero fatalities) to see how little this has in common with the "real world." *Schild's Ladder* also features this abstracted element. While factions disagree, there is no media coverage and no electorate that must be convinced one way or the other. In the end, decisions are reached by consensus, motivated by logic, and only barbaric anachronauts resort to violence to protest that consensual approach.

In *Clockwork Rocket* Egan places Yalda back in the rough-and-tumble of the academic practice of science and the societal aspect of engineering. At her university Yalda has to comply with the petty whims of the old guard in order to get the resources she needs. There are many who are less interested in the facts and experimental results than in protecting their pet theories and their turf. When she becomes involved in the effort to build a gigantic spaceship, there is political opposition from the wider society. Many people, and some of the media, mock their efforts (rather like Noah's neighbors making fun of the Ark). Even with the almost de rigueur eccentric rich guy backing the project, Yalda must switch from scientist mode to project-management mode, and eventually to political leadership. This is a difficult shift that few people make smoothly. There are personnel conflicts, sabotage, and logistical difficulties that must be managed. If one compares Yalda's challenges to the memoirs of those involved in the Apollo space project, it is easy to see the similarities. Enormous engineering projects rarely go smoothly, setbacks are almost guaranteed, and it is a huge challenge to keep all the participants, backers, media, and politicians happy, or at least keep them from actively undermining the project. It is rewarding to see Yalda tackle these challenges at all levels, even if it is unrealistic to see one individual filling all those roles. While all the societal interaction makes for a somewhat messier narrative, it is perhaps more satisfying than the abstractedly pure environment in which Roi operates.

ALTERNATE COSMOLOGIES

Egan is not the only science fiction writer to play around with the rigorous consequences of fantastic physics. Given Egan's notorious lack of in-person appearances, some wags have speculated that Ted Chiang and Greg Egan are one and the same (after all, like Clark Kent and Superman, they have never been seen together), and when one compares their themes and approaches (if not their styles), that joking proposition is tantalizingly tempting. Even the story note to Ted Chiang's story "Understand," in *The Hard SF Renaissance* says: "It is interesting to compare and contrast this story to Greg Egan's explorations of intelligence and personality in 'Reasons to Be Cheerful'—both Egan's and Chiang's stories are concerned with futuristic treatments for neurological damage with striking results" (Hartwell and Cramer 2002, 699). Chiang rose to prominence in a similar time frame to Egan, winning the Campbell Award for Best New Writer in 1992, although he was more of an "overnight" success, with his first published story, "Tower of Babylon," being nominated for a Hugo and winning a Nebula in 1990. Chiang tends to write about fantastic universes but ones that operate with their own rigorous and consistent sets of rules. He then ruthlessly interrogates those rules and their implications, and he sometimes features characters who are scientists in their own worlds, even when those worlds have much different physics than our own.

Critic Gary K. Wolfe has been overheard to remark that Ted Chiang and Greg Egan may be the only hard SF writers writing today, and while that is using a perverse meaning of the term "hard SF," it is worth some thought. Chiang and Egan share a concern with science for science's sake—not the technology we get from science, not esoteric quantum mechanical mysticism, not even abstruse metaphysics, but simply what science can tell us, and how that opens up the universe to humanity and vice versa.

Consider Chiang's "Exhalation" (2008), winner of the Hugo Award for best short story in 2009. It describes the life of people living in a world completely enclosed by walls of chromium. The air that fills this world consists of pure argon. The people are immortal automatons, made of titanium, with brains full of fluttering gold leaves. Their every movement is powered by air pressure. They have lungs full of pressurized argon, which they discharge over the course of a day, and they install fresh lungs each night. The narrator is an anatomist, which is a very limited field when everyone is immortal and the rare fatal accident generally leaves little to examine. However, when discrepancies start to crop up between (purely mechanical) clocks and the internal timekeeping of the people, he decides to take the classic SF step of experimenting on himself. (Note that this description uses "he" as an unfortunate default—the narration of the story is all in genderless first person, and there is no mention of, nor need for, gender among these people.)

In a scene that deserves to be immortalized as one of the most enduring images of science fiction, the researcher arranges a series of prisms, microscopes, and mechanical actuators, and dissects his own brain. He is the first to realize that it is differences in air pressure, not simply the presence of air, that powers life, and that everything unique about a person's brain is captured in the momentary patterns and currents of airflow through the brain. Hence, if ever a person lets their airflow run out, they do not become themselves again when new lungs are installed—the patterns that constitute consciousness are already lost. He quickly realizes that the reason people's internal timekeeping is slowing down is that the air pressure of their atmosphere is rising. Basically, air has been moving from a pressurized reservoir into their chamber but eventually the pressure differential will narrow, the system will reach equilibrium, and all life there will cease. This is exactly equivalent to how entropy works in our universe.

The pocket universe of the story is described entirely with references to incorruptible metals: the chromium walls (chromium is corrosion-resistant, and is added to steel to make it stainless), the titanium bodies of the people, the mercury running through the clocks, and the gold leaf fluttering in their brains. Even the argon that powers them is an inert noble gas. Chiang makes the point that even without the decay that we typically think of in connection with entropy (for example, rotting and rust), when everything reaches a state of equal energy, nothing can happen anymore. All the dynamism that animates a world will be gone.

Chiang's writing style is very different from Egan's. "Exhalation" has a certain formality of style, justified by the fact that the anatomist is inscribing words meant to be read by hypothetical explorers from another chromium pocket universe who may happen across his world after all life has ceased. Chiang uses a similar approach in a story titled "Seventy Two Letters," which is set in a version of Victorian England where the sort of kabbalistic magic that was once thought to be able to power magical golems is the reality of the world. In that story, the style is dictated by the times, and both of these stories share a certain stylistic tenor with the older SF of Robert Louis Stevenson (*Dr. Jekyll and Mr. Hyde*) and Jules Verne. The self-dissection scene in particular has the Jekyll/Hyde hallmark of a scientist experimenting on himself, although this time to wondrous rather than monstrous ends.

The anatomist of "Exhalation" shares much in common with the alien protagonists of *Incandescence*. Officially, both are motivated by the potential extinction of their species—spiralling into a black hole on the one hand, or suffering the pressure-driven equivalent of heat death on the other. "Seventy Two Letters" also shares this trait; when the scientists culture and examine the homunculi that live in sperm (in that universe, sperm really do contain miniature fetuses that grow into babies only when implanted in a female's ova and imbued with the animating life force contained therein) they come to realize that the human race will only be able to reproduce for a further five generations. However, in all these cases the protagonists are driven by their own curiosity well before discovering the threat, and in fact the threat is only revealed in its full extent through their investigations. The anatomist has had his self-dissection experiment in the back of his mind but had not been willing to risk it before hearing of the irregularities of the clocks; Zak is initially trying to validate the information on a map that he found in a library; and Robert Stratton of "Seventy Two Letters" spends idle time in his childhood trying to work out the limits and rules of the kabbalistic "names" that can animate different forms of golems.

Likewise, all of these stories spend more time on the investigations than on traditional character development. Stratton is fleshed out to an extent typical of a short story, but the anatomist of "Exhalation" is never named, and as we have discussed, Zak and Roi have more important things to do than engage in interpersonal drama. These are all characters that, strongly motivated by that quality we choose to call "curiosity," seek out important information that can help save their worlds. However, even in "Exhalation," when there is no wriggling out of the fate that physics has in store for them, the narrator experiences little disappointment, at least not compared to the wonder he feels at being able to discover so much about himself and his world. He addresses the hypothetical reader, presumably an explorer from another world: "I hope that your expedition was more than a search for other universes to use as reservoirs. I hope that you were motivated by a desire for knowledge, a yearning to see what can arise from a universe's exhalation."

"Exhalation" and *Incandescence* may be two of the purest dramatizations of the scientist's drive and yearning for wonder that have been written in science fiction. Both walk the reader step by step through the understanding of an alien world, toward a greater understanding of the underpinnings of our own world—entropy is at the heart of Chiang's story, and general relativity is at the heart of Egan's. However, Chiang's is clearly the more successful, because of its brevity, its style, and because entropy is a more accessible topic for the general reader than relativity. It is much easier to see where he is going with the story and to make the connection with our reality than it is with Egan's *Incandescence*.

Chiang's fiction often has concerns that parallel Egan's. Even in a story like "Exhalation," which focuses primarily on the macroscopic notion of entropy, there are also questions about mechanical intelligence. The anatomist is able to examine his own brain while he is still conscious, a similar notion to Egan's "Mister Volition," although without the existentialist angst. He discerns that his brain and its memories are made up of the patterns of air flow instead of, say, a written set of sequential memories and instructions: "The lattice was not so much a machine as it was a page on which the machine was written, and on which the machine itself ceaselessly wrote." The idea of consciousness as pattern instead of script underlies both "Learning to Be Me" and *Permutation City*. And both authors choose to show us strictly materialist universes. Much as Andrew Worth in *Distress* confronts his own mortality and the fact that his soul will not go on, the anatomist realizes: "I do not delude myself into thinking that this would be a way for me to live again, because I am not that air, I am the pattern that it assumed, temporarily. The pattern that is me, the patterns that are the entire world in which I live, would be gone."

Chiang has said, "Science seeks a type of explanation different from those sought by art or religion, an explanation where objective measurement takes precedence over subjective experience. And though hard SF can take many different forms, it always describes people looking for or working with that type of explanation" (Hartwell and Kramer 2002, 699).

BEAUTY, ELEGANCE, METAPHOR

An important point to remember is that in Egan's fiction, discoveries in math and science are beautiful things in and of themselves, even removed from their social context. Sometimes the stories deliver and explain this sense of awe and wonder about the universe effortlessly and to a wide audience. When David Hartwell attempted to define hard SF, the first criterion he chose was "Hard SF is about the beauty of truth . . . about the emotional experience of describing and confronting what is scientifically true" (James and Mendlesohn 188).

Consider this vignette from *Schild's Ladder*. Tchicaya, age nine, is worried about his future. If he is going to live for thousands of years, growing and changing the whole time, how will he know that he is still himself? His father sits down with him and reassures him using a mathematical parable. Imagine that you have an arrow with a specific length and direction (a vector), and without being able to measure absolute length or angles, you want to carry it with you such that it never changes length or direction. This is possible, over any different kind of geometrical space, using a series of steps known as a Schild's Ladder. Tchicaya is initially very reassured by this possibility, until his father shows him that if you build a Schild's Ladder along path B instead of path A the arrows you end up with are angled differently, even though in a very real sense they are both still the "same" as the arrow you started out with. The young boy is distressed by this variability, but his father points out, "Whatever happens, you can always be true to yourself. But don't expect to end up with the same inner compass as anyone else. Not unless they started beside you, and climbed beside you every step of the way" (251). It neatly illustrates that as you choose different paths through life, the person you turn out to be will be subtly changed compared to what alternate choices may have brought.

This is an elegant metaphor, and one of the few mathematical concepts illustrated by diagrams in that book (*Incandescence* has only two diagrams and could have used more; *Clockwork Rocket* and *Eternal Flame* each have plenty). The notion ties in with Egan's overall concern for the integrity of personal identity throughout his body of work—no wonder that this particular bit of mathematics lends the title to the book. Also, it highlights one of Egan's particular and peculiar strengths: almost certainly, there are other mathematicians out there who would agree that the concept of a Schild's Ladder is a beautiful and elegant construct in its own right. But how many of them would use that as a metaphorical foundation for musings on identity and life journeys, and be able to dramatize it as well? No matter how unlikely one might find the concept of using mathematics to reassure a little boy facing an early existential crisis, by the end it is easy to fall into something of a reverie meditating on the fact that even such abstract concepts as vector mathematics can help create a narrative of human life.

CHAPTER 5

SCIENCE AND SOCIETY

In *Eternal Flame*, one character mentions "the most powerful engine of change in history: people arguing about science" (361). The vast majority of Egan's writings concern science and the scientific process. Even when pointing out all the ways things can be unfair or go wrong, his fiction reflects a shining optimism that through the advancement of science the human race can achieve wonders. To say that this is not a universally shared faith would be an understatement. Scholars from many different intellectual backgrounds have challenged science's status as the preeminent mechanism for knowledge gathering and human advancement. This criticism has taken many forms, from the dogmatically religious to the abstractly postmodern. Throughout the 1990s a number of these attacks were widely publicized, and Egan's fiction did not shy away from engaging with the arguments in both satirical and emotional ways. One of his strongest stories, "Oceanic" (which won the Hugo Award for best novella in 1997), is his most autobiographical story to date and speaks to the religious impulse with some sensitivity. Although the science / anti-science debates continue to rage over topics such as climate change and evolution, since the turn of the century Egan has largely left the field. In the new millennium his fiction has focused on more elegant thought experiments rather than on the culture wars.

This chapter will look at how Egan's fiction has engaged in these culture wars over the years on the side of science and the rationalist, materialist universe. It will look at the role of myth in fictionalizing science, those Egan stories that directly engage with religion and morality, and those which directly engage with the postmodernism of the academy. Finally, it will look at science as a source of purpose and meaning, one which is not often credited by scientific doubters.

DIRECTLY ADDRESSING SCIENCE VERSUS RELIGION

> There are people who think that if you ask the question "Why is there something rather than nothing?" then the only meaningful answer is "God." I can understand why they feel that way, but I don't think that's really an answer at all. (*Gigamesh* interview, 1998)

When Egan's stories directly confront religion and religious themes, it is safe to say that religion and thought patterns based on faith do not fare well. In the late 1990s, Stephen Jay Gould proposed a resolution to the science / religion conflict that came to be known as "Non-Overlapping Magisteria." This idea proposes that science and religion need not step on one another's toes; science can concern itself with the empirical universe, all that can be directly observed, and religion can wrestle with the moral and ethical realm of being human and existing in human societies, as well as the "larger" issues of deriving meaning for our lives in the universe. Egan's fiction firmly rejects that concept. His stories show science and the scientific worldview as lending meaning to the universe in a completely different way than religious ideology, with the answers provided by religions leading to absurdities and sometimes unethical behavior.

"The Moral Virologist" has already been mentioned, reminding us that it is morally indefensible to create a virus that targets people one regards as "sinners" in an attempt to exercise God's will. "Our Lady of Chernobyl" is a very different story for Egan, having a thriller / detective-style plot slightly reminiscent of *The Da Vinci Code* ten years later. A small icon from the Ukraine depicting the Madonna has gone missing, the courier shot in the head. The narrator is hired to try to recover the icon. As he travels across Europe in his search, the detective has some time for sightseeing and philosophical pondering. "Arcane theological disputes between people as alien to me as the ancient Egyptians had transformed the entire continent—along with a thousand purely political and economical forces, for sure—but nevertheless, modulating the development of almost every human activity, from architecture to music, from commerce to warfare, at one level or another" (*Luminous* 264–65), a good reminder that one cannot simply ignore religion even if one is not particularly religious. Its influence spreads far and wide across history as well as across contemporary politics.

The icon referred to in the title is a portrait done in the classic Russian style, but with paint which has been mixed with a small amount of spilled fuel from the Chernobyl meltdown. It is believed by many to have been inspired directly by the Virgin, which makes people willing to pay exorbitant sums and even kill for it—the final body count is three, which is high for an Egan story. The story is a bit of a muddle, much less clear-cut than is typical for Egan.

> I sat on the rubble with my head in my hands. I couldn't pretend that I didn't know what the icon meant to its rightful owners. I'd seen the church they were building, the place where it belonged. I'd heard the story, however apocryphal, of its creation. And if talk of divine compassion for the dead of Chernobyl being channeled into a radioactive Christmas card was meaningless, ludicrous bullshit to me, that wasn't the point. De Angelis had believed none of it, but she'd still blown her job, she'd still gone to Vienna of her own free will. And I could dream of a perfect, secular, rational world all I liked, but I still had to live, and act, in the real one. (*Luminous* 287)

"Unstable Orbits in the Space of Lies" (1992) is a rare Egan story in which the fantastic premise is not scientifically supported (although it is rigorously developed). In this story, the world has been overwhelmed by geographical regions devoted to different ideologies. Literally, what you believe in depends on where you stand. In this scenario, all kinds of beliefs, not simply religions, are treated similarly. Political beliefs and various brands of rationalism acquire enclaves of their own. The narrator has been carefully walking around the edges of these regions, trying not to get permanently sucked into any single belief system. He behaves very much like a particle orbiting around a complex system of gravitational attractors, trying to keep enough momentum such that he is never trapped in a stable orbit around a single large body. This future is effectively post-apocalyptic, as the infrastructure is decaying and the narrator is more or less a tramp. On the day of the change, everyone was gripped by wave upon wave of mystical revelation, being wrenched from faith system to faith system every few seconds. The narrator likens the experience to an intense bout of gastroenteritis, which is a scenario and metaphor that Egan uses again in *Distress*.

"Unstable Orbits" describes the experience of being taken hold of and released by different belief systems, each of which seems beautifully and perfectly *true* at that moment, in that place. Just by walking, the narrator recapitulates the age-old conflict between Christian faith and the rationality of science. He walks through the transcendent glory and comfort of God's perfect love, through moderate doubt, to pure rationality, then to over-the-top solipsism and finally to nihilism, all in the course of a page. "The last few minutes' confusion still rings in my head, satisfyingly jumbled, the giddy succession of truncated epiphanies effectively cancelling each other out, leaving nothing behind but an amorphous sense of distrust" (*Axiomatic* 334). In the end, the narrator fears that even the freedom-loving life of struggle and doubt that he has been living is just another belief system that has caught him up, one that is geographically spread into paths instead of stable locations. The thought that his life free of attractors is just another attractor is almost too much for him to bear. Can we ever know how many of our thoughts and beliefs are "our own" and how many are "merely" the result of unexamined assumptions and faith? Throughout it all, of course, there is still an "I," a solid core of personality that has free will to act. In this way, "Unstable Orbits" mirrors the set-up of "Axiomatic," where people can purchase different belief systems via nanotech, but none of those belief systems negates the responsibility imposed by having free will.

In "Mitochondrial Eve" (1995), discussed earlier, a cult that seeks to use scientific results to unite humanity and ease intertribal warfare instead spawns a countermovement that encourages violence. Also appearing in 1995, "Silver Fire" overflows with vitriol for people who increase human suffering by shoehorning real things into an ideological framework and applying them willy-nilly. There is a sense running through these stories that when science is hijacked for religious purposes, it is demeaned in some way and will never yield positive results. In fact, there is an implication that almost any kind of ideology or religious-style belief will inevitably lead to conflict, pain, and suffering.

The Silver Fire of the title is a new infectious disease that flays its victims from the inside out and makes them feel like they are being burned alive. There is no known cure or vaccine. The only treatment is to embed the victims in a Jell-O-like anesthetic polymer with nutrients piped in and wastes piped out. Like many infections with high fatality rates, it does not have a high transmission rate, so it has not reached pandemic levels. However, epidemiologists keep close tabs on it. One of these epidemiologists, Claire, is the narrator of the story.

She finds a subculture of traveling dance parties in which virtual beings shining with silver light are shown (through wall-sized TVs) walking the "Trail of Happiness" to undo the "Trail of Tears." The visualization references Silver Fire because, according to an adherent, "Their bodies are frozen, so their spirits are free to walk the Trail of Happiness through cyberspace for us! Didn't you know? That's what Silver Fire is *for*! To renew everything! To bring happiness to the land! *To make amends!*" (*Luminous* 202). Claire, of course, finds this appropriation of intense suffering completely abhorrent, even more so when she learns that certain individuals have been deliberately spreading the disease in order to encourage more people to walk the "Trail of Happiness." This story blatantly stacks the deck against the fuzzy thinkers, but there is no doubt that True Believers (and some scientists) have done worse things in the name of the Higher Good of their faiths.

Silver Fire is the sort of out-of-the-blue disease that is the hardest for people to understand emotionally. Claire wants to tell the victims' families:

> *It just happened. People suffer like this for no reason. There is no sense to be made of your son's ruined life. There is no meaning to be found here. Just a random dance of molecules.* (*Luminous* 185)
>
> [. . .]

At some level, we still hadn't swallowed the hardest-won truth at all: *The universe is indifferent.* (*Luminous* 190)

Perhaps one of the least prescient near-future scenarios in an Egan story is in this one: "And if Christian fundamentalism wasn't exactly dead and buried, its power base had certainly gone into decline; the kind of ignorance and insularity it relied upon seemed to be becoming almost impossible to sustain against the tide of information" (*Luminous* 185–86). The story sees organized religion declining, replaced by the fuzzy thinking of spirituality. "Silver Fire" also acknowledges the ease with which mystical thinking seems to win the PR war, over and over:

> [In] a heated debate on *The Reality Studio* . . . A freelance zoologist from Seattle named Andrew Feld spoke first, putting the case that Silver Fire "proved beyond doubt" his "controversial and paradigm-subverting" S-force theory of life, which "combined the transgressive genius of the Maya and the latest developments in superstrings, to create a new, life-affirming biology to take the place of soulless mechanistic Western science."
>
> In reply, virologist Margaret Ortega from UCLA explained in detail why Feld's ideas were superfluous, failed to account for—or clashed directly with—numerous observed biological phenomena, and were neither more nor less "mechanistic" than any other theory which didn't leave everything in the universe to the whim of God. She also ventured the opinion that most people were capable of *affirming life* without casually discarding all of human knowledge in the process.
>
> Feld was a clueless idiot on a wish-fulfilment trip. Ortega wiped the floor with him.
>
> But when the nationwide audience of students voted, he was declared winner by a majority of two to one. (*Luminous* 204)

Note that here is a (presumably) white male taking the flaky pseudoscience side and a (presumably) Hispanic woman taking the Enlightenment position. This is seen again in the debates in *Distress*. As mentioned in chapter 2, the stories very carefully make the point that scientific values need not be culturally dependent and that they can be immensely empowering for people from non-Western countries and cultures.

"Oracle" is a very rare excursion into historical territory, with a twist that allows Egan to dramatize the science-versus-religion position explicitly.

Robert Stoney is a gay scientist and mathematician in England, a clear stand-in for early-twentieth-century genius Alan Turing, inventor of the modern computer and code-breaker extraordinaire of World War II. Egan lifts a quote directly from a schoolmaster under whom Turing suffered: "This room smells of mathematics! Go out and fetch a disinfectant spray!" When Robert's homosexuality comes out, he is pressured into doing intelligence work for the British government. Blackmail leads to fears of blackmail, and eventually he is labeled a national security risk and imprisoned. In real life, Alan Turing was convicted of being gay and his court sentence was the imposition of estrogen hormone treatments to dampen his libido. Sometime after the treatments ended, he was found dead in his house. At the time his death was ruled a suicide, although debate continues as to whether his death was suicide, accident, or foul play.

In contrast, Robert Stoney is rescued from his prison by a time/world traveler, someone who is going back to alter different world-paths (she cannot alter her own past due to paradoxes) and trying to create a better future. In Robert's world she is hoping that prompting him and giving him some hints and encouragement will accelerate the technological advancement of the twentieth century.

Robert's adversary in the story is John Hamilton, professor at Magdalen College and creator of the "Kingdom of Nescia," a dead ringer for C. S. Lewis. The Nescia/Narnia stories value faith and steadfastness above all else, particularly the unshakable faith of a child, and this is the worldview that is most at odds with the spirit of scientific inquiry. Egan plays up Hamilton's snobbish ignorance of mathematics and science. He also dramatizes the role that Hamilton's faith plays in helping him deal with his wife's cancer. In sections written from each man's point of view (although overall the novella has a third-person narrator) we see how they each view the world filtered through completely different mindsets. Hamilton sees everything, even very negative experiences, in terms of God's plan for his life. Stoney, on the other hand, takes the world as it is and revels in gaining understanding of the underpinnings of the universe.

With the help of the time traveler, Stoney is able to make rapid advancements at the cutting edge of several fields; Hamilton visits his lab and is shown an MRI, new breeds of disease-resistant plants designed from the DNA up, new vaccines, plus some primitive AI. Hamilton regards Stoney's accomplishments as sheer arrogance and hubris. He accuses Stoney of being a Satanist taking inspiration from the Devil. Stoney angrily denies this in explicitly atheistic terms. Hamilton is especially horrified by Stoney's meddling with the natural order, in everything from genetic engineering to robotics.

> "You're plotting to overthrow nature, bending the world to the will of man."
>
> Stoney sighed. "Not at all. More refined technology will help us tread more lightly. We have to cut back on pollution and pesticides as rapidly as possible. Or do you want to live in a world where all the animals are born as hermaphrodites, and half the Pacific islands disappear in storms?"
>
> "Don't try telling me that you're some kind of guardian of the animal kingdom. You want to replace us all with machines!" (*Crystal Nights and Other Stories* 210)

This is similar to the attitude of the aliens in the Orthogonal universe (resistance to "meddling with nature"), although in that trilogy no religious faith is involved. As Egan says, talking about the Orthogonal books in an interview, "Philosophically, this seemed like a perfect opportunity to explore the naturalistic fallacy: the idea that whatever nature has produced is the way things should be. In our own society this is sometimes bound up with religion, but I don't think that's the only way it arises. So, although these aliens have no religion, many of them do take the attitude that nature provides a kind of ideal template for life, and their role is to accommodate to that, not to fight it" (Burnham interview).

Hamilton decides to debate Stoney on stage, in a live television broadcast, and Stoney agrees. The set topic, "Can a Machine Think?" isn't ostensibly religious but instead goes back to one of Egan's core concerns, machine intelligence. Hamilton uses Gödel's incompleteness theorem to argue that machines, building consciousness from doing nothing but arithmetic, can never be fully sentient because they will never be able to use pure arithmetic to understand themselves; no system can ever be 100 percent consistent and 100 percent complete. Stoney responds by pointing out that right now, computers cannot learn from experience; all they have is brute-force numbers. Of course machines can't think like a person. But once they can, then we will be able to compare their minds with our own.

The real debate, however, comes later, backstage. Stoney tells Hamilton everything about the multiverse of parallel worlds, the ones in which things are improved, where his wife's cancer could be cured. Hamilton rejects him stoically. At the very end, a version of Hamilton from one of these happier universes comes to offer him a chance to move to a better place, although it would basically mean acknowledging that Stoney (secularism) was right and that Hamilton (religion) was wrong. Considering this visitation to be a vision of temptation sent by the Devil or by God to test him, Hamilton also rejects this most secular version of salvation. In fact, the future version of Hamilton/Lewis does a very poor job of trying to convince Hamilton to renounce his faith. He references a scene in Nescia/Narnia that is explicitly about clinging to faith even when there is no hope of proof or reward. And he speaks of sending Joyce's children, Hamilton's stepchildren, back to their father. In real life, the first husband of Joy Davidman Gresham, Lewis's wife, was an abusive man, and Lewis would have done just about anything to make sure the boys did not go back to him.

The alternate Hamilton says: "There is no Devil. And no God, either. Just people. But I promise you: people with the powers of gods are kinder than any god we ever imagined." And: "I can't promise you Heaven. We have no disease, we have no war, we have no poverty. But we have to find our own love, our own goodness. There is no final word of comfort. We only have each other." And: "The real world is richer, and stranger, and more beautiful than anything ever imagined. Milton, Dante, John the Divine are the ones who trapped you in a drab, grey underworld. That's where you are now." For Hamilton/Lewis, most of these promises would have sounded very much like the temptations that the snake offered Adam and Eve in the garden, especially in offering knowledge that will make man like God.

"Oracle" seems to imply that that science can deliver a better world and that religion can only offer suffering. The counter argument is that people are people, and they make the world one way or the other; neither atheists nor true believers have a monopoly on cruelty or kindness. Certainly, in "Oceanic" Egan presents a more nuanced view of a variety of approaches to religious observance. Overall, the position these stories collectively take is that ideology is particularly dangerous when it allows people to justify causing other beings to suffer—whenever it blinds people to the suffering that they are causing in others or themselves. This could be through stoking tribal divisiveness or deliberately infecting people with a disease or committing murder to further a cause. It is clear that in this view, almost anything that causes or increases human suffering is anathema, and no ideology should be able to countenance it. In a few early stories, Egan levels his own criticisms at the practice of science, especially when it comes to experiments involving living creatures. "Demon's Passage" has an intellectually enhanced lab animal railing against its own fate; the celebrity eugenicist in "Eugene" is a quack bilking money from the hopeful and gullible; the lack of informed consent for the placebo protocol in "Blood Sisters" means that one twin dies without knowing what drug (or lack thereof) she was being given. Even in the classic story "Learning to Be Me" it is revealed that the medical industry has removed some inconvenient checks and balances and that the neural network technology is not as faithful as advertised. However, there seems to be a feeling throughout his stories that the "pure" sciences, far removed from messy biology and as free as possible from political meddling, can reach toward universal truths *without* increasing human suffering, in a way no other field of inquiry can.

In *Distress* the conflict is between science and any number of mystical and supernatural ways of understanding the universe. When it comes to religion itself, the narrator Andrew Worth has what might be called a reverse conversion experience while he is suffering (literally and intensely) from drug-resistant cholera. While he is lying in the hospital, both wanting to die and fearing death, he says:

> All I wanted to do was rise to my feet and walk out of the hospital, leaving my body behind. Flesh and bacteria could fight it out between themselves, I had lost interest. . . . And I finally understood, as I never had before . . . [that] this diseased body was my whole self. It was not a temporary shelter for some tiny, indestructible man-god living in the safe warm dark behind my eyes. (*Distress* 272)

He hallucinates a visit from a representative of the New Age "Humble Science!" group and tries to gain comfort and solace from some greater spiritual truth, but she has no answer when he demands to know how to ignore the physical reality which at that very moment is trying to kill him. He has a chat with the attending doctor, who happens to be an atheist who rejected the religion he had grown up with. The doctor says:

> Because there is no *abyss*. There *is no* yawning chasm waiting to swallow us up, when we learn that there is no god, that we're animals like any other animal,

> that the universe has no purpose, that our souls are made of the same stuff as water and sand. . . . I've stopped pretending that the things I value [such as kindness and charity] are locked up in some magical vault called "God"—outside the universe, outside time, outside myself. That's all. I don't need beautiful lies anymore, just to make the decisions I want to make, to try to live a life I think is good. (*Distress* 278–79)

Having come to grips with the most important fact he can think of—that he is part of the universe, and that this life and this material world is all there is—Andrew is finally ready to become an active driver in a plot wherein he had previously been a hapless observer.

It is important to remember that in our own history, science and religion have not always been antithetical. Many great scientific thinkers have been devoutly religious, from Newton (with his rather eccentric biblical and alchemical inquiries) to pioneers of electromagnetism such as Michael Faraday and James Clerk Maxwell. Even Egan himself spent the better part of a decade as a devoted believer, as chronicled in his autobiographical essay "Born Again, Briefly."

According to the essay, Egan grew up moderately Anglican. Just before he started high school, his older brother, whom he admired, took up Charismatic Catholicism. In nighttime discussions about religion and philosophy, his brother eventually persuaded young Egan to kneel and pray and accept the Holy Spirit.

> When I'd finished praying, I felt a great sense of contentment, but I wasn't actually sure that the crucial event had taken place. My brother assured me that it had, and the feeling grew stronger. When I silently prayed, my prayers were answered immediately by a powerful upswell of emotion, and this wordless dialogue became richer and more intense, until all I had to do was mentally invoke the name of Jesus and I felt overwhelmingly happy, safe, and loved. Within a matter of hours, I had gone from someone who would dutifully repeat the tenets of his religion, but might easily have been persuaded to reconsider them, to one who found it as absurd to question God's existence as to question the reality of the sun while lifting his face to the sky at noon. ("Born Again, Briefly")

This state lasted for several years. For a while he belonged to the same group his brother was part of, but he drifted away. He was never particularly doctrinal or ideological, but even as his studies of math and science intensified, he felt no need to question the reality of God and God's love.

> Given that I'd ended up with a faith that was perfectly compatible both with my own conscience and with anything the natural sciences might reveal, it might easily have lasted my whole lifetime. Having access to a sense of great peace and contentment, and a conviction that in the end all wrongs will be made right, is not a burdensome state to be in.
>
> Why, then, did it finally unravel? Very slowly, I turned my attention to the thing itself: the reason for my faith, the source of my conviction. What exactly had happened to me when I prayed beside my brother that night? What exactly was going on, each time I called upon the Holy Spirit?
>
> My faith didn't like to be scrutinised. When I asked myself these kinds of questions, the reply was a jolt of transcendental happiness and a reminder that I shouldn't expect to understand such things. But I was not part of any religious community; there was nobody around to reinforce the interpretation of the experience that had first accompanied it. I felt joyful when I prayed. This proved . . . what? Perhaps it simply meant that I'd discovered a way to feel joyful when I prayed. The human brain is a flexible organ, and compared to all the complicated trance states and meditative practices of other religions this seemed like a very modest achievement, something even a twelve-year-old child subject to the right kind of duress might manage.
>
> Nevertheless, I resisted that conclusion for years. A vague alternative explanation was not a disproof of my original interpretation—and even if someone could have put me in a scanner and pointed out every detail of some physical mechanism, what would that mean? That religious joy—just like every other kind of joy—had certain physical correlates. How was the Holy Spirit supposed to comfort me without laying a finger on my neurotransmitters?
>
> I don't recall any one thing that finally drove a stake through the heart of my faith. Perhaps it boiled down to a question of which was most likely: that I had been born into a culture that, out of all the many religions on Earth, happened to worship the true creator of the universe, or that I had put my own spin on an emotional Rorschach blot that could easily be explained without invoking anything supernatural at all. ("Born Again, Briefly")

This spiritual journey forms the core of the Hugo Award–winning novella "Oceanic." At the beginning of the story young Martin lives on a boat on a largely oceanic planet called Covenant. He knows that his ancestors were from Earth, that they had become Angels (the sort of digital posthumans seen in *Diaspora* and *Schild's Ladder*), and that they eventually decided to return to embodied living on this planet. His understanding of this is couched in the language of myth and scripture. His older brother Daniel has taken up with the Drowned cult of the Deep Church, and he persuades Martin to undergo a rather dangerous baptism ceremony, where he is weighted down and dropped into the ocean on the end of a line. As his oxygen supply diminishes, he passes through fear and panic and desperation before coming to the sense of religious transcendence and euphoria of belief. As his brother pulls him out of the water, he knows that the love of Beatrice, their goddess, will always be with him.

The Martin of "Oceanic" is one of Egan's most thoroughly realized characters, which makes sense, as the character shares so much history with the author. We follow Martin from this conversion experience, through his association with his brother's friends in the Drowned cult, how his feeling of being protected and guided by Beatrice colors his perceptions of events, both positive and negative, including his first sexual experience. The language and morals of Beatrice's faith mirror traditional Christianity in most ways. As he learns more about biology and the different interpretations of his planet's history, his core faith remains unchallenged. As Egan said in his essay, "The existence of God was a given, as much as my own existence. Science would continue to reveal whatever it revealed, and I had nothing to fear from that." As Martin studies more and also deals with his mother's death, his faith slowly drains away. His biological studies lead to neurochemistry, and he begins to parse out the biological factors that went into the transcendent conversion experience he had as a child. His results eventually attract media attention.

At one point he finds himself on a televised panel (the societal level of Covenant has rather conveniently reached that of our 1990s) with an anthropologist, a priest of the mainstream religion, and two devout adherents of two different gods. The two adherents band together to attack the anthropologist, who is claiming that all faiths are true to their adherents. Then Martin and the mainstream priest have the following exchange:

> "I'm perfectly happy with a God who resides within us," offered the Transitional theologian. "It seems . . . immodest to expect more. And instead of fretting use-

> lessly over these ultimate questions, we should confine ourselves to matters of a suitably human scale."
>
> I turned to him. "So you're actually indifferent as to whether an infinitely powerful and loving being created everything around you, and plans to welcome you into Her arms after death . . . or the universe is a piece of quantum noise that will eventually vanish and erase us all?"
>
> He sighed heavily, as if I was asking him to perform some arduous physical feat just by responding. "I can summon no enthusiasm for these issues." (*Dark Integers and Other Stories* 227)

Martin feels the loss of his faith keenly but realizes that he can live without it. In the end he confronts those who peddle the transcendent experience to the masses but fails to convince many people to give up their faith and hope.

POSTMODERN SILLINESS

In addition to its nuanced view of religion, "Oceanic" touches on another area of concern for Egan: the cultural relativism that was being widely debated in academia in the 1990s. "Oceanic" in 1998 and *Teranesia* in 1999 represent the height of Egan's disgust with that particular intellectual movement. Postmodern deconstructionism points out, rightly, that knowledge does not form in a vacuum. As much as any members of society, scientists operate within a culture that informs what questions they ask and how they interpret their results. Unfortunately, in the nineties especially, this was transformed into rather overblown rhetoric that claimed there was no such thing as an objective reality. It got out of hand to the point that even academic feminist theorist Susan Bordo asked in her book *Unbearable Weight*, "Is the postmodern merely a stylish, self-promoting, have-it-any-way-you-like fancy of contemporary intellectuals?" (279)—although she answers her own question in the negative. The movement became an attractive target for satire and understandably drew no little ire from Greg Egan.

In *Teranesia*, Prabir and his sister Madhusree go to live with their aunt after their parents are murdered. The aunt, Amita, and her ex-partner, Keith, are the targets of Egan's over-the-top satirical frustration with some of the intellectual fads among academics in the late 1990s. Consider:

> "How did you meet Amita?" [Prabir] asked innocently. . . .
>
> "It was at a performance space in the city," Keith began tentatively. "Twelve

> years ago." He frowned, struggling to dredge up the details. "The Anorexic Androgynes were reciting the Unabomber Manifesto, with backing music by Egregious Beards." He added helpfully, "They were a Country Dada band, but they broke up years ago." . . . "I'd already done a PhD in X-Files Theory at UCLA, and Amita was just starting her Master's in Diana Studies with the University of Leeds, via the net. U Toronto was in the process of opening its own Department of Transgressive Discourse—at last!—so it was only natural that we both applied for positions." (*Teranesia* 85–86)

Prabir, who has been raised by Indian skeptics and research scientists, finds all of this a bit bewildering. But he is astounded by Keith's description of Amita's research work:

> "Have you ever wondered why computers are so hostile to women?"
>
> "You mean . . . why do some men harass women on the net?"
>
> "Well, yes, but it goes far deeper than that. Amita's work not only reveals the fundamental reason for the problem, it offers a stunningly simple solution." He jabbed at the notepad with his finger. "Zero and one. Absence and presence. *And just look how they're drawn!* 'Zero' is female: the womb, the vagina. 'One' is male: unmistakably phallic. The woman is absent, marginalized, excluded. The man is present, dominant, imperious. This blatantly sexist coding underpins all modern digital technology. And then we ask ourselves why women find it an unwelcoming space!" (*Teranesia* 87–88)

Her solution is to reengineer a computer where all the zeroes are swapped for ones and vice versa, to be called a "transputer." Prabir is furious:

> Computers don't have little numerals inside them. . . . Zero is usually coded in memories by the absence of electrical charge in a capacitor, and one by the presence of charge. . . . There are no diagrams of vaginas and penises, or anything else to do with people's sex. . . . These are *Hindu-Arabic numerals!* People have used them for centuries; they have nothing to do with computers! If you really imagine that they're drawings of private parts, it's not technology that should offend you—it's mathematics! (*Teranesia* 88–89)

And indeed, Amita's work hopes to eventually overthrow all patriarchal mathematics and logic—"the old, male dispensers of truth." In the end, Prabir is despairing:

> He sat down, light-headed, still disbelieving. In the camp, when he'd recalled the things his father had said about Amita, he'd feared that she might be religious, but it was even worse than that. She was opposed to everything his parents had stood for: the equality of men and women, the separation of scholarship from self-interest, the very idea of an honest search for truth.
>
> And he'd delivered Madhusree into her hands. (*Teranesia* 90)

There is no denying that the practice of science has historically been male-centric. However, there is a difference between discussing how the "practice" of science has been hostile to women and how "science itself" is somehow patriarchal. In *Distress*, Violet Mosala's response to these sorts of criticisms is harsh. There's never any doubt where Egan's sympathies lie when it comes to issues such as this. One journalist asks Mosala:

> "It seems to me that your whole approach to these issues reflects a male, Western, reductionist, left-brained mode of thought . . . How can you possibly reconcile this with your struggle as an African woman against cultural imperialism?"
>
> Mosala said evenly, "I have no interest in surrendering the most powerful intellectual tools I possess, because of some quaint misconception that they're the property of any particular group of people: male, Western, or otherwise. As I said, the history of science is one of convergence toward a shared understanding of the universe—and I'm not willing to be excluded from that convergence for any reason." (*Distress* 129–30)

The postmodern cultural jargon also shows up in "Silver Fire" (1995) as academics seek to position the eponymous disease within a cultural zeitgeist and go overboard in doing so. And these same concerns are expressed through the character Janet Walsh in *Distress*:

> Janet Walsh was an award-winning English novelist—and one of the world's most prominent members of Humble Science! She'd first come to fame in the twenties with *Wings of Desire* ("a delicious, mischievous, incisive fable"—*The Sunday Times*), a story set among an "alien race," who happened to look exactly like humans . . . except that their males were born with large butterfly wings growing out of their penises, which were necessarily and bloodily severed when they lost their virginity. The alien females (who lacked hymens) were all callous and brutal. After being raped and abused by everyone in sight for most of the novel, the hero discovers a magical technique for making his lost wings grow

> back—on his shoulders—and flies off into the sunset. ("Gleefully subverts all gender stereotypes."—*Playboy*) (*Distress* 103)

Egan challenges this emotional and political approach to truth seeking: "Followers of Mystical Renaissance only want the truth if it suits them, if it *induces the right emotions*. If they were honest, they'd just stick a hot wire in their brain at whatever location made them believe they were undergoing a constant mystical epiphany—because in the end, that's all they offer" (*Distress* 137). Part of Egan's disdain for people seeking truths outside of the realm of science seems to come from a feeling that they are being intellectually lazy. As we have seen from many of his stories, he has no problem asking readers to work hard for commensurate rewards. One of Mystical Renaissance's slogans is "TO EXPLAIN IS TO DESTROY," which neatly sums up the antithesis to the theme of almost every Egan story.

Once again, we return to Violet Mosala. She points out that while cultural concerns influence the progress of science (for instance, how one defines "simplicity"), that does not mean that scientific searches for truth functions on the same basis as religious searches for truth:

> Suppose every human being was wiped off face of the planet tomorrow, and we waited a few million years for the next species with a set of religious and scientific cultures to arise. What do you think the new religions would have in common with the old ones—the ones from our time? I suspect the only common ground would be certain ethical principles which could be traced to shared biological influences: sexual reproduction, child rearing, the advantages of altruism, the awareness of death. And if the biology was very different, there might be no overlap at all.
>
> But if we waited for the new scientific culture to come up with their idea of a TOE, then I believe that—however different it looked "on paper"—it would be something which either culture would be able to show was mathematically equivalent in every respect to our TOE . . . just as any physics undergraduate can prove that all forms of Maxwell's Equations describe exactly the same thing. (*Distress* 128–29)

Over and over, *Distress* returns to these themes—what science is doing is drastically different from what religion is doing, and scientific understanding is critical for humans as individuals and as a species.

CRITICS OF "PURE" SCIENCE

The 1990s saw many criticisms leveled at science as a discipline. Consider the following statement from Mary Midgley in *Science as Salvation* (1992). She was concerned that many public scientists, such as Freeman Dyson, were spinning wild tales of immortality and surviving the end of the universe, potentially positioning themselves and humanity as godlike beings. In the course of refuting their fantastic rhetoric, she wrote about many aspects of scientific philosophy that seemed troubling. "The ideal of objectivity which we are considering asks scientists, then, both to be objective themselves—in the sense of being fair—and to believe that nature is objective, in the sense of lifeless, inert, and without any tendency to pattern" (49). That sentence would make a practicing scientist pull her hair out, since everything that science does is based on the universe being rich in patterns. Almost certainly Midgley and the average scientist mean different things when they use the word "pattern," and that sort of misunderstanding exacerbates the problem of communication across disciplines.

Another example of cross-discipline criticism is seen in this introduction to a serious paper published in 1985, titled "Science: A Masculine Disorder?":

> Science is based on the professional creation and certification of knowledge which is tied to powerful interest groups, notably the state, corporations and the scientific profession itself. Patriarchy is based on male control of dominant social structures and the exclusion of women from positions of power through means such as direct discrimination, socialisation and the gender division of labour.
>
> Patriarchy within the scientific community is manifested through male control of elite positions and various exclusionary devices. The scientific method incorporates masculine features such as the objectification of nature. Scientific knowledge is masculine in its neglect of women's experience and its adoption of paradigms built on assumptions of competition and hierarchy. (Bowling and Martin 308–16)

These paragraphs start off entirely reasonably, but then they extend the argument too far (from the perspective of the scientist) in attacking the underlying scientific method and declaring that scientific knowledge must always and forever be ineluctably masculine.

Egan was hardly alone in his frustration about the rhetoric surrounding postmodernism and criticisms of science in the 1990s. After all, this was the same decade that saw the Sokal Hoax, where in 1996 physicist Alan Sokal wrote a paper filled with nonsense about quantum gravity, entitled "Transgressing the Boundaries: Towards a Transformative Hermeneutics of Quantum Gravity," and submitted it to *Social Text*, a journal of postmodern cultural studies, which promptly published it and lauded it as an achievement in cross-disciplinary studies. The waves from that controversy reverberated in the science and humanities communities for years afterward.

Overall, the best way to make sure that science is not purely Western and patriarchal is to get as many people as possible around the world involved in its practice. Bias can never be eliminated in any one individual. Everyone swims in the sea of culture and that inevitably affects everything we do, including the practice of science. How research is conducted, what questions are asked, and what receives funding will all be carried out under the shadow of blind spots, privilege, and prejudice. However, because of the scientific method, where hypotheses are testable and experiments replicable, even gross errors of judgment and bias can eventually be straightened out. Medical textbooks were historically quite vague on questions of women's health, especially menstruation and pregnancy. However, as more women have entered the medical and biological fields, asking different questions and carrying out wide-ranging research programs, the situation has improved. One problem with all the postmodern silliness outlined above is that it added to the (numerous) forces discouraging women and people of color from entering scientific and mathematical fields in Western countries.

The limits one perceives in the practice of science depend to an extent on what one is trying to do. In 1966, Abraham Maslow, then professor of psychology at Brandeis University, wrote, "As a philosophical doctrine, orthodox science is ethnocentric, being Western rather than universal. It is unaware that it is a product of time and place, that it is not an eternal, unchangeable, inexorably progressing truth" (*Psychology of Science* 1). Maslow specifically argues that the methodology promoted by the "hard" sciences is inadequate in addressing the more holistic understanding of human experience needed by his field, psychoanalysis. But in a broader sense he worries that "our orthodox conception of science as mechanistic and ahuman seems to me one local part-manifestation or expression of the larger, more inclusive world view of mechanization and dehumanization" (2). While Maslow finds that frightening, much of Egan's sense of wonder is rooted squarely in a world that is mechanized without becoming dehumanized (depending on whom you ask). Maslow also points out that the pattern of repeated abstractions and generalizations that works so well in physics is inadequate when dealing with human psychology. It is certainly a source of some worry and trepidation when the characters in *Permutation City* start talking about the short cuts and simplifications made in the software modeling humans in a virtual space. Artificial neural networks can allow a system to model complex phenomena that are not well understood, but not everyone will want to entrust their psychology or their soul to such a system.

In Egan's universe, there is nothing that is not amenable to scientific inquiry. Many people throughout history have disagreed with this view or found it threatening. As John Passmore notes in *Science and Its Critics* (1978), "Kierkegaard was happy to let science deal with plants and animals and stars"; but, Kierkegaard wrote, "to handle the spirit of man in such a fashion is blasphemy" (2). Midgley criticizes people like Egan: "They glorify *Homo sapiens* as the sole centre of value in a universe that exists merely to support him, and they ground that value primarily on a special use of the intellect, on the fact that human beings do science" (73). Certainly it is true that Egan's characters see the universe as having no deeper meaning than what humans (or other beings of the same level of intellect; many of Egan's "posthumans" are actually "postaliens") ascribe to it or find in it. However, contrary to Midgley's claims, that in no way stops the characters from finding "reverence, awe and sympathy for the world that we enquire about" (Midgley 73). The sense of wonder that is perhaps a secular alternative to religious awe is found throughout Egan's fiction and is heavily dependent on observing and understanding the universe as it is and only ascribing meaning to the facts post hoc. Midgley sees scientists as objectifying and thus disrespecting nature, but one can argue that Egan's fiction has immense respect for nature as it is, as opposed to what people might want nature to be. It may be that some scientists completely cease to have respect for the subjects of their study, but that attitude is not necessary or even common.

Another objection arises regarding science's assumption that the universe is made up of inert and uncreative or soulless matter. There is no doubt that this view of the universe has given tacit permission for the ruthless exploitation of nature upon which the nineteenth-century industrialists and their heirs embarked. However, science may be more neutral in this respect than commonly imagined. In more recent times scientific findings have resonated well with the imagery and concerns of the environmentalist movement, even while still viewing nature as being fundamentally material and soulless.

It is fair to point out that science sometimes gets things drastically and hilariously (or tragically) wrong, and this wrongness often comes from the cultural blinders that surround nearly every working scientist. For instance, here is the considered opinion of noted neurologist Dr. Charles L. Dana, writing in the *New York Times* in 1915 (as quoted in Cordelia Fine's 2010 *Delusions of Gender*):

> There are some fundamental differences between the bony and the nervous structures of women and men. The brain stem of woman is relatively larger; the brain mantle and basal ganglia are smaller; the upper half of the spinal cord is smaller, the lower half, which controls the pelvis and limbs, is much larger. These are structural differences which underlie definite differences in the two sexes. I do not say that they will prevent a woman from voting, but they will prevent her from ever becoming a man, and they point the way to the fact that woman's efficiency lies in a special field and not that of political initiative or of judicial authority in a community's organization. There may be an answer to this assertion, but one cannot deny that the mean weight of the O.T. and C.S. in a man is 42 and in a woman 38, or that there is a significant difference in the pelvic girdle. (131)

Certainly, desire for a specific outcome encourages researchers to fudge data, ignore contrary results, or simply make inferences where no reasonable interpretation exists. At this point the scientist runs the risk of not playing fair and not accurately reflecting reality. Scientists insist to themselves and to others that they are "objective" (even when they clearly are not)—because they have to be in order to have any hope of accurately reflecting reality. However, even when an individual or team goes down an entirely wrong path, science has self-correction mechanisms that other forms of epistemology lack. We know that past scientists were wrong because later scientists turned up new evidence, and eventually the weight of the evidence is enough to overturn the older misconceptions. Egan goes to great lengths to dramatize this iterative process of science, especially in stories such as "The Planck Dive" described in the introduction of this book. And reality eventually always wins out somehow. After all, "Reality is that which, when you stop believing in it, doesn't go away" (Dick).

Science is often perceived as elitist, as beyond the ken of normal folks. In *Science and Its Critics*, Passmore notes the difference between older and newer technology: "A steam engine, as compared with a diesel electric, has indeed something *human* about it. It generates metaphors, like 'letting off steam'; it has inspired poetry. We can learn, or envision ourselves learning, how to repair such inventions. We admire the manual dexterity of a watch repairman or a plumber but have no disposition to feel that he posses magical powers" (36). Compared to this, much modern technology consists of black boxes that can only be fixed by a technological elite who use other black boxes to fix the problem. Consider the frustration of many in the maker/do-it-yourself/hacker culture with today's smartphones; even if you were able to crack open the case without destroying the thing, what could you hope to learn or fix or change? "[N]owadays it is precisely as magic that science appears to a great many citizens. . . . as occult, taught through mysterious initiations, handed on in a very exclusive filiation. Its generation of an elite is one reason why we so often find it alleged against science that although it purports to give human beings power over nature what it really does is to give certain human beings power over others" (Passmore 37).

This notion that scientists and technologists are the high priests of arcane and occult knowledge is one that Egan's stories deliberately set out to dispel. Over and over he argues and tries to show that this body of knowledge is understandable, even the most complex and counterintuitive results of quantum physics and general relativity. In the same way that he rejects those who do not interrogate the received wisdom of religion, he wants us to see that there is nothing in scientific knowledge that we cannot interrogate and understand for ourselves. The fact that he encounters so much resistance in this project (critics complaining that it is too hard, too dull, or requires an "entrance exam") highlights how entrenched the sense of science as a "hard" topic fit only for the scientific elite has become in our culture. The esteem in which Egan is held by the science fiction community also places his work within the narrative of the scientific elite, the high priesthood of which deigns to share tidbits of discoveries with the masses.

Of course, science also sometimes seems to throw up boundaries to human ambition. "That is one cause of resentment against science. It often says: 'That is impossible.' A witch doctor or a 'spiritual healer' never tells his patients that there is absolutely nothing to be done; magical powers know no limits except more powerful countermagic" (Passmore 29). There is certainly some frustration engendered by the fact that with the laws of physics, we are up against some hard-and-fast boundaries. No fast-talking Ulysses can persuade the gods to tilt things in our favor anymore. This was the thrust of Tom Godwin's 1954 short story "The Cold Equations," wherein a young girl who has stowed away on a ship, which is carrying the bare minimum of fuel, must be ejected and killed so that the ship can complete its life-saving mission. Egan's universe is even colder than Godwin's—absolutely everything is the result of the most rigorous, mathematically based physics possible—yet his humans and posthumans live lives of joy, fulfilment, and discovery, with no little adventure and drama.

MODELING REALITIES

As science has progressed through the centuries, our understanding of the universe has changed with it. Where once we saw a well-ordered universe of intricate but predictable mechanisms, now we see a universe full of chaos and probabilities. It no longer makes sense to describe our world in terms of clockwork; instead, we use the language of information and statistics. While Hal Clement may have personified the storytelling of a well-ordered universe with his stories set on enormous planets with specific engineering challenges, Egan represents hard science fiction that has completely embraced all that modern physics has to offer.

Many simple systems can be described with simple equations—a thrown ball follows a ballistic trajectory. But with the addition of something as simple as wind resistance, the equations become nonlinear and difficult to work with. How much this is seen as a problem depends on the application; even on windy days, a batter can still hit a pitched ball. However, as systems become more complex and intractable, it often makes sense to model or simulate the system on a computer to get a feel for how it behaves under various conditions.

Many science fiction stories can be described in this way, as models or thought experiments. Changes to technology, society, or the universe are posited and then dramatized. These changes can be as simple as the introduction of a new strain of flu, as dramatic as the end of the world, or as complex as a galaxy-spanning space empire. Egan has been lauded as a unique voice and talent during the last two decades of science fiction—in part because of the rigor with which he develops his consequences and in part because of the physics on which he bases his thought experiments.

In *Permutation City*, which is perhaps the most discussed of his novels, Egan imagines that humans can be scanned and the copies can live in digital environments. This was not a new idea in 1992, as much of the cyberpunk of the 1980s had been concerned with various levels of mind/machine interface. However, Egan works through the consequences in a different way. He opens the book by showing that being a software construct means that one's software can run quickly or slowly, or be run out of order or in parallel, all without changing one's perception of self. This is a vertiginous feeling, one that opens up the reader's understanding of what would be involved in the simulation. He also goes into the details of what things would be simulated at high resolution and what would be done sloppily or with shortcuts in order to save processing time. Finally, he walks through several different permutations of what someone could do with a personality-editing ability combined with functional immortality. When you combine that digital existence with an existential threat of cosmological destruction, as in *Diaspora*, we get a novel full of beings who can modify themselves to perceive shapes in higher dimensional space and who find life that exists within biologically simulated environments.

More than that however, it is the science and technology that Egan chooses to examine that set him apart. Even with his first widely read novel, *Quarantine*, he chose to dramatize a particular interpretation of the wave-function collapse in quantum mechanics—not simply the ever-popular many-world interpretation, but something more subtle and arcane. In *Schild's Ladder* a change imposed on the space-time structure of the universe grows and converts our relatively empty space-time into a much richer soup. "Luminous" and "Dark Integers" imagine discontinuities in the mathematical rules of transastronomical numbers. *Incandescence* works out the orbital dynamics of an asteroid orbiting a black hole pursued by another stellar object, and the Orthogonal universe changes the rules of space-time itself and then works out the consequences in everything from optics to quantum mechanics. No one, not even the deans of hard SF such as Hal Clement and Gregory Benford, have ever attempted to conduct thought experiments based on such abstruse ideas and worked them out with such rigor.

The extent to which these stories succeed for any given reader is a function of their inclination and tolerance. After writing a scathing review of *Incandescence* (to which Egan responded with "Anatomy of a Hatchet Job") Adam Roberts reviewed *Clockwork Rocket* in the form of a dialogue between the part of his brain that admired what *Clockwork Rocket* was doing and the part of his brain that was bored stiff. The entire piece is well worth reading, but here are some telling excerpts:

PRŒGAN: At the heart of all of this is science, and the scientific method in its most appropriately sciencefictional form—the thought experiment. Tolkien is praised by critics for creating an entire parallel human culture, including background history, languages and customs; but Egan has achieved something more capacious, more ambitious and considerably more impressive: not only an entire alien biology and society, but an entire new kind of physical universe. There isn't another SF writer capable of it, I think.

ANTEGAN: Clotted with diagrams and equations, dense to the point of frank indigestibility, this is a novel that grows grey with the breath of Scientist discussing endlessly with Scientist about Science. Indeed, at places the novel reads almost like a radical experimentation in anti-art, an exercise in seeing how much raw intellectual weight the load-bearing walls of aesthetics (let's say, "character," "style," "form" and "image") can stand. . . . It lacks grace, it evinces neither charm and wit, it is not stylishly done.

PRŒGAN: We can retrace the steps Einstein trod, and get some, second-hand sense of the thrill he must have experienced discovering an entirely new physics. But Egan gives us the chance to do more than that; because his physics is newly minted for this imaginary world, and this means—if only we are ready to make a little effort—we get to experience the excitement of discovery (as it were) first hand! . . . You're saying it bored you. I reply: saying so reveals a great deal about you, and very little about the novel.

ANTEGAN: No! Well, yes . . . it did bore me. And I'm not proud of that reaction. But that's not really the basis of my objection. SF strikes me, necessarily, as an ironic mode of art—its relationship to reality is not mimetic, but neither is it entirely arbitrary or disconnected (we would hardly care about it, if so). . . . [*Clockwork Rocket*] is as unironic a novel as I can think of. (Roberts 2012)

This dialog dramatizes the tension at the point that Egan's words on a page find a reader. In bringing the scientific sensibility to science fiction, in writing about characters who are scientists, in writing clearly and prosaically so as not to lose readers who may have difficulty with the subject matter, Egan's fiction suffers the same critiques leveled at science itself: dull, boring, inhuman. However, there are other readers for whom Egan personifies all that is best about the scientific and humanistic endeavor: the sense of exploration and of wonder, reveling in our unparalleled ability to understand the universe we live in.

SCIENCE AS PURPOSE AND MEANING

One finds several powerful statements about science's role in our hearts and minds in Egan's fiction. At the end of *Incandescence*, when Rakesh and Parantham find the alien race they are looking for, they discover a society so drastically incurious that they can barely get anyone to talk to their obviously artificial robot ambassador. This is contrasted with the vibrant communal efforts of that same alien race when their world is at stake, when understanding the relativistic universe in which they live becomes essential for ensuring their survival.

Roi finds the practice of science enthralling and almost addictive: "Instead of being blissfully content with the same healthy crop at the end of each shift, she could only claim success now from something new: a revelation, a contradiction, a twist that turned their old guesses inside out. . . . If they ever did reach the end of the mysteries of weight and motion . . . she did not know how that second part of her would go on living" (*Incandescence* 166).

As reporter Andrew Worth explores the society of Stateless in *Distress*, he is invited to an informal ritual experience for new immigrants. Stateless is a new island, completely manmade, grown from bioengineered coral. Near the shoreline there is a large shaft kept open through which people, wearing scuba tanks, can be lowered into the sea beneath the island. They travel through a cross section of the island and are able to see and feel exactly how the island works. They can feel the wind from the organisms in the rock that make gasses that keep the island afloat. Directly underneath their feet, the ocean erodes the island out from under them and the island is constantly renewed. "That's what holds the island up: just a fine mist of calcium, fading away into the depths, and a few trillion microscopic creatures whose genes tell them what to do with it" (*Distress* 170).

> This was what the people of Stateless had in common: not merely the island itself, but the first-hand knowledge that they stood on rock which the founders had crystallized out of the ocean—and which was, forever, dissolving again, only enduring through a process of constant repair. Beneficent nature had nothing to do with it; conscious human effort, and cooperation, had built Stateless—and even the engineered life which maintained it couldn't be treated as God-given, infallible; the balance could be disturbed in a thousand ways. . . . All the elaborate machinery had to be monitored, had to be understood.
>
> In the long run, discord could literally sink the place. . . . And if it was naive to think of this understanding as any kind of panacea, it had one undeniable advantage over all the contrived mythology of nationhood.
>
> It was true. (*Distress* 171–72)

Later, after Worth's atheistic revelation at the hands of a nasty strain of cholera, this passage resonates with his discovery: "I'd hit bottom. Once you'd touched the bedrock of the underworld, the foundations of the universe, there was nowhere else to fall" (*Distress* 281).

Throughout his oeuvre, we can see the role in which Egan places scientific understanding. Without science, humanity will always be at the mercy of poorly understood forces, and even if we wrap those forces in the narrative cloak of myth they can still destroy us. With a thorough understanding of the universe and how forces act within it, we can take control of our own destiny. It is an immense responsibility, but one with commensurately large rewards.

Perhaps even more emphatic is the story "Glory." In the opening three pages, travel from the Amalgam to a backwater planet is described as a straight-up, far-future engineering marvel involving the quantum Zeno effect, relativistic time dilation, transmission of a pattern through a shockwave in a star, and finely tuned orbital dynamics. The researchers who have just completed this grand traverse are interested in the archaeology of a long-dead race that contented itself with the pursuit of higher mathematics. At the end of the story, one of the researchers has found the result of that past race's efforts, a triumphal result that ties together many otherwise disparate branches of mathematics. She tries to communicate this to her colleague before being shot down, but her partner does not get all of her message. The tablets she found were destroyed. The surviving researcher thinks up another feat of interstellar engineering, paralleling the one that opened the story, that might allow her to reconstruct her friend's last message and the ultimate answer in mathematics—but she decides to let it pass. Based on the expectations set up by the opening, we imagine that the protagonist will leap at the chance to use the black hole that is conveniently at hand to "solve the problem" and avoid losing this beautiful and valuable mathematical knowledge. By declining to use that solution, she reminds us that the joy of intellectual inquiry is in the process itself as much as it is in the ultimate answer. She declines the offered shortcut to satisfying answers, deciding instead to prolong the process of intellectual exploration and curiosity. While there is no doubt that the same result will be found eventually—discoverable things rarely remain undiscovered—she feels that there is no point in shortening the journey, which is, in the end, more important than the destination. "If we really are going to live forever, we'd better stay curious if we want to stay sane" (*Axiomatic* 310).

INTERVIEW WITH GREG EGAN

KAREN BURNHAM: What sort of science fiction did you read growing up?

GREG EGAN: Because my mother worked in a library, I managed to get an adult library ticket at the age of about nine or ten, so I was reading all the SF that was around in the early '70s. If you name any SF writer who was in print then, I probably read at least one thing by them, but don't ask me to list all the titles. I was reading one or two novels a week, year after year, so I was just immersed in this vast soup of SF tropes, like a bacterium picking up genes from plasmids.

Certainly Clarke and Asimov would have been among the earliest names that I knew to look for; I remember that by the time *The Gods Themselves* reached the library I was already a long-time Asimov fan. And I have fond memories of reading Dick's *Eye in the Sky* and *Counter-Clock World* at about the same time.

KB: Were there any nonfiction books or series that you picked up as a young reader that were equally influential?

GE: I would have been reading maths and science books at the same time, but by now I have no memories of any titles except for the magazines: *Scientific American*, *Sky and Telescope*, and *Electronics Australia*. I had some chemistry sets, a microscope, and a telescope—I tried to grind my own telescope mirror, working from a book, but I couldn't get it right, so my parents bought me a small refractor.

KB: Some of your earliest published short stories are horror rather than SF. What attracted you to write horror initially?

GE: My first couple of published stories, "Artifact" in 1983 and "The Way She Smiles, the Things She Says" in 1985, were SF, and the third, "Tangled Up," was a sort of fantasy. I had a run of three horror stories after that. But I also wrote countless unpublished SF stories, starting in my teens and all the way up until the late '80s. I couldn't tell you who I got my first rejection slip from, what the story was called, or even what it was about—I would have been 13 or 14, and all the details have vanished into my mental slush pile.

I enjoyed reading horror when I was young, mostly short stories in anthologies. I don't recall many authors or titles, but I remember being creeped out by something I'm fairly sure was one of Lovecraft's when I was about 10. My three published horror stories were all based on dreams, and I'm still reasonably happy with them, but I never really developed that kind of style and mood into anything more substantial.

KB: When you do research for your books these days, what sources do you turn to?

GE: Textbooks, the arXiv, Wikipedia, Google Earth. Of course Google Earth isn't perfect—the images can be out of date, or difficult to interpret. When I went to Iran to research *Zendegi*, I discovered that some locations I'd initially chosen for protests in Tehran had changed from open squares into construction sites.

For a certain kind of hard SF, the nice thing is that you can usually check everything by consistency as well as against published sources. I used a few general relativity textbooks when I was writing *Incandescence*, so whenever I calculated something that was mentioned explicitly in one of those books, I could be sure I'd got it right; but for all the other results I needed, there were usually at least three different ways I could analyse the situation, so if I got the same answer by every route, I could be fairly confident that I hadn't made a mistake along the way.

KB: You've obviously done an amazing amount of work in understanding physics as part of the research and background for your books and stories. Have you ever been tempted to go into academia and study these concepts formally on the graduate level?

GE: I didn't really embark on any substantial study on my own until the mid-'90s, when I taught myself general relativity, and that didn't leave me pining to return to university; if anything, it made it clear that I'd be far happier just satisfying my curiosity at my own pace. And I doubt that any PhD thesis could be half as much fun, or as wide-ranging, as the work I did for the Orthogonal books.

KB: Between the publication of *An Unusual Angle* and that of *Quarantine*, cyberpunk came to prominence. Did you read any of the cyberpunk authors at the time, and did they have any noticeable impact on your writing?

GE: I read *Neuromancer* in 1985, because I was voting for the Hugos that year and I thought I ought to read all the nominated novels. I really hated it; aside from the style and the characters, which definitely weren't to my taste, a lot of things about the technology in the book seemed very contrived and unlikely, especially the idea that anyone would plug in a brain-computer interface that they knew a third party could use to harm them.

Over the next few years I read some Rucker and Sterling novels, which I definitely enjoyed more than Gibson. So there was some reasonable stuff written under the cyberpunk banner, but none of it felt very groundbreaking to anyone who'd been reading Dick and Delany, and if it hadn't been wrapped in so much hype I probably would have enjoyed it more. In fact, the way cyberpunk as a movement influenced me most was a sense of irritation with its obsession with hipness. I don't think there's much doubt that "Axiomatic" and the opening sections of *Quarantine* have a kind of cyberpunk flavour to them, but my thinking at the time would have been less "Maybe I can join the cyberpunk club!" and more "Maybe I can steal back private eyes and brain-computer interfaces for people who think mirror shades are pretentious, and do something more interesting with them."

KB: A lot of your fiction focuses on biotech, specifically neuroscience. How did you come to be interested in that field? Do you approach the research for those stories differently?

GE: Biology and neuroscience in particular turn the abstract, philosophical fact that humans are matter like everything else into a tangible set of insights and possibilities. Just knowing that we're some kind of collection of molecules only gets you so far; we're a very specific kind of thing, so if you're interested in what it means to be matter, the biological sciences are enormously important. If you want to know where love, morality, kindness, jealousy, fear, and joy actually come from, the answers are all biological.

I don't have any formal education in biology, so when I write a story about biotech or neuroscience, I read around the subject as much as I can and just try not to make a fool of myself.

KB: In stories like "Axiomatic" and "Reasons to be Cheerful," we see how many of the elements we consider central to our identities can be controlled by neurochemistry. Similarly there are many software-based characters in your fiction who can edit aspects of their own personalities. Throughout it all the characters still have a sense of "I" that is responsible for the choices they make regardless of the influence of neurochemistry—but when the protagonist of "Mister Volition" goes looking for that "I," it's not there to be found. What are your thoughts on the way we construct identity given the organic influences of our brains and the potential for fine control of computerized brains?

GE: Identity is not irreducible or immutable, but our biological history has left us with a situation where it makes sense that we're not wildly unstable or incapable of any kind of internal consensus. I mean, we only have one body and it can only do a limited number of things at a time, so all our different drives and priorities have to sort out some way to get along or we'd just be paralysed. It would also be very counterproductive, in evolutionary terms, if we couldn't predict our own future behaviour at all. For a social animal living in a complex environment, there's a tension between the benefits of flexibility and the pitfalls of being completely erratic.

So I think a sense of identity is our way of reflecting on the particular consensus we've achieved and making judgements on how well it's worked in the past and what we expect of it in the future. In the end, I'd say my identity consists of all the things about my personality and values that persist—some because they're impossible to change in any practical sense with the means at my disposal, and some because I wouldn't change them even if I could. Of course the "I" making this judgement is just the same bundle of things that's being judged, and they all have some kind of physical cause, however complicated it might be. And the various things in that bundle fight with each other or reinforce each other through means that are ultimately physical means—whether they're doing it entirely within the brain, or whether they're doing it by getting the body to take actions that will have some effect on the balance of power.

Now, I don't actually know how stable that whole setup would be if we were given vastly greater powers of self-modification. Even if we had tools for the job that did precisely what they claimed to do, it's difficult to say in advance where it would lead. Maybe most people would just trim away a few petty neuroses and unwanted bigotries, and end up simply becoming slightly nicer versions of themselves. Or maybe we'd all end up as useless hedonists or raving megalomaniacs. Even if the tools won't let us damage ourselves so badly that we cease to be sentient at all, there are a lot of ways it could go wrong.

KB: You've written frequently about how consciousness may affect reality on various levels. Given the way the science has developed over the years, what are your current thoughts about this topic in the "real world?"

GE: I've always believed that the most plausible position is what might be called the standard materialist view of consciousness: the human brain is matter just like any other matter, and consciousness is simply a property of the brain. That we're conscious adds nothing to our ability to act upon the world that can't be accounted for, in principle, in terms of the ordinary behaviour of the molecules from which we're composed.

In fact, I think that's one of the most important insights of the last three hundred years: human beings belong entirely to the material world, and we're ultimately amenable to the same kinds of investigation and manipulation as any other physical system. Sometimes this is in the foreground of my work—in stories such as "Reasons to be Cheerful" and "Axiomatic"—but even when it's not, it's usually implicit in the technological infrastructure, as it is in *Diaspora* and *Schild's Ladder*.

I did write three books that violated that basic assumption to various degrees, though the idea in *Quarantine* wasn't really connected with consciousness per se; the hypothesis was that the human brain contained a neural structure that was somehow capable of collapsing a superposition of quantum states to a single eigenstate. This wasn't posited as a side effect of consciousness itself, and the system that did this could as easily have been located in the kneecap or the liver as in the brain.

I didn't believe this was at all plausible when I wrote the book, I just thought it was a fun idea. If there's any kind of collapse, it most likely happens purely at random, or as a result of some threshold being crossed in terms of the energy or the number of degrees of freedom of a system. But the evidence seems to favour the absence of any collapse at all; it seems more likely that the "collapse" is just how things look when a quantum system becomes entangled with something you can't access. If you can only make measurements on part of an entangled system, the results obey the laws of classical probability rather than exhibiting quantum interference.

I think the idea in *Permutation City* belongs to the same class of theories as Max Tegmark's proposal (1998) that every single mathematically coherent structure that would contain observers is real—there's no extra "fire" that needs to be breathed into the equations, you just need the equations to imply the existence of someone who gets to experience what that particular universe is like.

There are variations on this idea, where rather than talking about mathematical structures you talk about every possible algorithm—not because there's meant to be some cosmic computer running those algorithms, but because if we assume that anything an observer could possibly experience would be computable, then enumerating every computer program lets you enumerate, as a subset of those programs, every possible sequence of experiences.

Anyway, this is a fun metaphysical area that people are continuing to think and write about, but I don't believe it's something that's ever going to be amenable to scientific testing. Even to make a novel out of this, you really have to cheat a bit—not just in assuming that the idea is true, but also in choosing what to tell, and in breaking the rules to make things more interesting. If your hypothesis is "Every possible conscious experience finds itself in the dust" . . . what is there to say? It's the ultimate exercise in scene selection to extract something that dramatizes that idea.

Distress put aside the idea of a multiplicity of universes and focused on the anthropic principle in its starkest form: the fact that when we're trying to explain anything, our own existence is where the process really has to start. We don't reason "The Big Bang happened, and that caused X and Y and Z . . .," we reason "I know A and B and C, which leads me to believe X and Y and Z." To dramatize that, in the novel I have the laws of physics being up for grabs, with human factions battling to choose the Theory of Everything. I don't believe that's remotely plausible, so it's not a matter of science ever supporting such a scenario. It's just one way of meditating on the strangeness of the position we're in, where in a sense we can imagine that the universe might have turned out to be completely lifeless . . . but in another sense we really can't.

Of course there have been theories around in particle physics for decades which suggest that our own universe might contain billions of different regions where the local details of the physics at low energies are different. That's a much less metaphysical proposal, because in principle we might eventually obtain direct experimental evidence that one of those theories is true. Then we'd be able to shrug off any sense of the laws around us being especially suited to life or consciousness, in the same way we shrug off any sense of Earth being especially hospitable: it's just a matter of there being a huge amount of variation in all the relevant parameters.

KB: In "Singleton," you take care to explicitly rule out Roger Penrose's notion of consciousness as a quantum phenomenon. What is your take on the science of quantum mechanics as it relates to human minds?

GE: I don't believe that quantum phenomena play any special role in the human mind.

It's a little bit tricky to phrase this claim precisely, because obviously we live in a universe governed by quantum mechanics, not classical mechanics, and all of chemistry would stop working if quantum mechanics didn't apply. It might even be that some surprisingly large-scale and long-lived coherent quantum states are important in biology; I think there's some evidence for this in photosynthesis, and when it comes to humans, some interesting claims about the way our sense of smell is able to determine the shapes of molecules, in which it might turn out that a quantum effect called tunneling plays a role in the receptors of our olfactory neurons. That's quite controversial, but I don't think it's absurd, and it could be that there are many other situations like that throughout biochemistry.

There are limits, though, as to how large and complex a system can be at body temperature and still exhibit quantum effects. Everything we know from physics, chemistry, and biology suggests that a neuron is a "classical system": quantum mechanics is essential in order to understand how its smallest parts work, but once you get above the length scale where you need to do quantum chemistry, it can be understood with classical laws. A neuron certainly can't be in a quantum state of simultaneously firing and not firing, which is the scale on which one neuron influences another. If every movement of my muscles—which includes every word I speak, and every action I perform, however subtle the psychological processes behind those actions—is ultimately due to neurons operating as classical systems, I can't see any reason to believe that there's anything else going on that's essential to the way our minds work.

People sometimes argue that there could be some ineffable subtlety to our consciousness that lies below the level of neurons firing—some quality we can't put into words, but which would be absent without quantum phenomena. But I don't think that claim makes any sense. Every aspect of our subjective experience has some potential to influence what we do; even if I can't communicate to you exactly what my mental state is at some moment, the very fact that I might say "I can't describe this feeling" is a consequence of that state. So however "private" our inner lives, they can't be divorced from our behaviour, and we don't say or do anything without neurons firing and sending signals to our muscles. Anything going on inside our skulls that is too subtle to affect the behaviour of neurons is also too subtle to comprise any part of our minds.

KB: In *Schild's Ladder*, the characters are distinctly posthuman. Even the embodied people are physiologically far removed from today's humans. Was there a particular method you used to assign gender pronouns to the various characters? Was there a specific reason that you chose not to return to the asexual pronouns that you used in *Distress*?

GE: In *Distress* (and even in *Diaspora*) there were people with conventional genders as well as those without, so I used the genderless pronouns to distinguish the two cases. In *Schild's Ladder* ancestral gender dimorphism has completely vanished, but I wanted to avoid making a big deal of that, so I thought it was better to use a translation into present day English that sounded as natural to the reader as possible. In *Distress* when there's an asex character, that's strange and significant to the protagonist, so it's OK to do something with the language that jars and brings attention to itself. On reflection I'm not sure that it was the right decision to keep using those pronouns in *Diaspora*, and to be honest I'd grown a bit sick of them by the end of that book!

As for assigning gender pronouns to the characters in *Schild's Ladder*, I just matched them to the names, and I chose the names because I liked the sound of them.

KB: In the stories in which people are able to exist in digital forms, I don't recall any instance of computer viruses or other errors creeping into the architecture running all the programs. In your view, how could such a future stay immune from the sorts of malware that we're familiar with in our own day and age?

GE: The problems we currently face from both sloppy programming and malicious software have more to do with historical, commercial, and social factors than any deep, inescapable facts of computer science. Of all the computer crashes and security breaches to date, I suspect about three quarters are due to trivial things like buffer overflows. More modern computer languages and programming practices already make those kinds of errors much rarer, but there's still an enormous scope for improvement, ranging from mathematically rigorous verification of computer code to the adoption of completely different architectures than aren't as brittle as the current designs.

In the very long term—the *Schild's Ladder* or *Diaspora* time frame—when we've completely rebuilt all the hardware and software infrastructure many times over, and when their robustness and security are life-and-death matters for most of the population most of the time, I'm quite sure there'll be no systemic freezes and crashes, or low-level viruses. But at a sufficiently high level, of course things can always go wrong in some fashion. In *Diaspora*, there are no crashes in which the virtual environments disintegrate or the polises go haywire and need to be rebooted, but nobody knows if the Orphan being grown in the first chapter is going to be a reasonably well-adjusted sentient being or something dysfunctional that needs to be erased.

KB: If scanning technology were currently available and the kinks were all worked out, would you choose to upload yourself?

GE: I have no philosophical objection to becoming an upload, in principle, and if you're asking mainly about identity issues, personally I'm not terrified of the possibility that I'd run amok with the editing tools and turn myself into someone I'd hate.

But in terms of ever actually doing it—if it came along sometime in the next fifty years or so—I expect that would depend very much on the context. If it was the province of billionaires, say, and I happened to win a lottery, I'm not at all sure I'd leap at the chance. Or to take the other extreme, if most uploads lived a precarious existence as digital serfs, that wouldn't be too attractive either.

KB: Your posthuman fiction avoids the SF tropes of computerized hive minds or the Singularity. What are your reasons for avoiding these areas?

GE: I can imagine an alien species where something akin to an ant colony possesses a mind, while the individual denizens of the colony do not, but I can't imagine why our descendants, digitized or otherwise, would ever wish to turn themselves into anything similar. We might come up with vastly improved tools for collaboration and communication, but that's not the same thing at all.

I haven't actually read many works that use the trope of "computerized hive minds," but it seems to me that it's just a fantasy based on a false analogy: that you can somehow combine a multitude of human-level intelligences into something that is "as much more sophisticated" than a single human as a hypothetical intelligent ant colony is more sophisticated than a single ant. But the phrase "as much more sophisticated" is just empty verbiage; it doesn't actually mean anything to say "X is to a human as a human is to an ant." If you want X to have some ability that humans don't have—not even humans with access to massive amounts of computing power—you need to spell out precisely what that ability is and why it should arise in that context.

The Singularity, at least as Vinge envisions it, is based on the same kind of false analogy. It's uncontroversial that if we could be digitized, there's a lot of scope for our minds to be made faster, more efficient, and less prone to various kinds of errors, but I see no compelling reason to believe in Vinge's notion of "transcendence," in which there are types of consciousness that are superior to our own in a qualitative fashion that goes completely beyond those forms of improvement.

In fact, I'd say humans crossed the point about thirty thousand years ago when we gained the capacity to reason well enough to understand any physical process whatsoever, given enough time and patience. We're completely unchanged biologically from our Stone Age ancestors who could barely count, but every year hundreds of thousands of seventeen-year-olds are learning enough quantum mechanics to calculate the orbitals of hydrogen atoms. Even if our descendants remained entirely unmodified, they'd be perfectly capable of making the same kind of advance, over and over again.

As an SF reader, I thought the idea of the Singularity was very entertaining the first few times I encountered it, in Vinge's novels, but I think it's been flogged to death by other writers since then. And I'm certainly not persuaded by people who believe that the Singularity is going to happen in real life, though I suppose that depends on exactly how it's defined. I do think AI of some form is inevitable, eventually, and it's important to debate the ethical issues and the dangers that potentially arise from that. But I think people who believe in what Vinge calls "Applied Theology"—the creation of AIs with essentially God-like powers, who will either solve all our problems or enslave us—are just deluded.

KB: In many space-opera-style universes, you find all sorts of galaxy-spanning wars and accompanying imperial politics. The characters in the far futures of *Schild's Ladder* and *Incandescence* (the Amalgam) seem to avoid all those sorts of pursuits and distractions. How do they arrive at a future free from war and (most) politics?

GE: In the long term, technology has the potential to make radical changes to the costs and benefits of any form of violence or coercion. If a person ends up being a piece of software that can be backed up to a billion different specks of dust spread over a trillion cubic light years, how hard will it be to kill such a being, or even seriously inconvenience him? And what exactly would your dispute with that person be, if all of your own needs could be sated with some infinitesimal fraction of the galaxy's physical resources?

Of course you can posit cultures, or even immortal individuals, who are committed to exponential growth in their resource use, but since this can't be sustained in the long term—the speed of light means the raw territory anyone can acquire can only grow cubically with time—ultimately that's just a recipe for misery and frustration. Natural selection has left us with some drives and dispositions that work against our restraining our own growth, but some of these are almost trivially easy to circumvent, as with contraception, and in time we might choose to make deeper changes to our psychology that allow us to be content with the kind of restrictions that would forestall conflict long before we hit any purely physical barriers to growth.

In *Schild's Ladder* there is quite a bit of politics, though, because something exceptional has come along that's shaking up the physical situation on which the culture has come to rely.

KB: "Oracle" is a rare foray into historical territory. Why did you choose Alan Turing and C. S. Lewis specifically to have that debate?

GE: "Oracle" is one of those stories that is the product of all kinds of chance elements. My initial aim was to write an anti-Faustian tale about technology, partly out of frustration at the widespread cliché that humans are so flawed and technology so corrupting that it can only lead us into ruin. So the basic idea of a time traveler bringing advanced technology from the future came from that, and then the traveler's motives and the issue of many-worlds quantum mechanics led me to give her a special kind of artificial brain (the Qusp, which ultimately made its way into both the prequel, "Singleton," and *Schild's Ladder*). But once I decided to have the traveler seek out an alternative version of Turing—as someone with an artificial brain might well do—the story became much more about that character, Robert Stoney, and the way his life turned out differently from Turing's.

An alternative C. S. Lewis seemed like the obvious choice for a contemporary antagonist with a very different worldview. Some readers have complained that the character of Hamilton in the story doesn't accurately reflect Lewis's attitudes to science, but I changed the names deliberately to indicate that I wasn't trying to create portraits of any real historical figure. Once you change a single thing you're not talking about the same person any more, and the story's not at all about what the real Lewis or Turing "would have done" in various counter-factual circumstances.

KB: Similarly, *Zendegi* was a return to near-future SF after novels such as *Schild's Ladder* and *Incandescence*. Why did you choose to set that story in Iran?

GE: I'd just spent five years in the company of people from the Middle East and South Asia, to the point where it would have felt peculiar and unnatural not to write something about that region. I wasn't interested in writing a depressing story about the plight of refugees—I'd already got the impulse to do that out of my system with "Lost Continent"—and the most plausible location for a story with a real science-fictional component was Iran, which is a technologically advanced country with a highly educated population.

I'd read a bit about the 1999 student demonstrations in Tehran as part of some work I did trying to help an Iranian man who'd been involved in those protests (and who was locked up in Australia for more than five years when he came here seeking asylum), and it struck me that the overthrow of the ayatollahs was definitely a matter of "when" rather than "if." But I didn't want to get too bogged down in that, because Iranian politics are eye-wateringly complicated and the details aren't all that interesting. So I decided to make the revolution, essentially, a farce, starting with the pious Guardian Council member caught in a car crash with a transsexual prostitute, and keeping the bloodshed to an absolute minimum. A more realistic story of the collapse of the regime might have taken up an entire book twice the length of *Zendegi*, but this was always just meant as a prelude to establish the context for things that happen later. Nevertheless, I think it captures something genuine about the spirit of the movement and the Iranian culture. In 1999, when the university dormitories were attacked by militias, ordinary people in the surrounding suburbs intervened to help the students, and that's an image that really stuck with me and fed into many of the scenes in the first part of the book.

KB: Are you still involved in refugee issues? Has there been any improvement in recent years in Australian treatment of refugees?

GE: Things got better for a while, but now they're bad again. By around 2005/2006, all the people who'd been locked up for as long as six years were finally released, and children were no longer being detained. When there was a change of government in 2007, the incoming Labor Party had a policy that sounded wonderful on paper, in which they said that detention should be used for the shortest possible time and only as a last resort. But they never actually put that into law, and now there are all kinds of long-term detainees again, including people who have been classified as refugees but given adverse security assessments, so they can neither be deported to their country of origin nor released into the community. There have been a lot of suicides in detention this year.

I'm not involved in any significant way at the moment. Once you make a serious commitment to an issue like that the demands it makes on your time are almost limitless, and my experience from 2002 to 2006 was that I found it almost impossible to get any writing done. I'd befriended dozens of people who were in very bad situations and needed a lot of support, I was making six or eight trips to remote detention centers every year, and I had people staying in my house who'd been released with no right to work and no income. So I had very little time or mental space left over for writing, and I was living off rapidly dwindling savings and occasional Japanese translation deals.

Right now, I'm on a series of very tight deadlines, and I'm being paid about a third as much per book as I used to get in the '90s, so my only real choice is between leaving this round of the fight to other people, or giving up writing completely and becoming a refugee activist with a day job in computing.

KB: In a world with any number of worthy political causes, what was it about the refugee situation that motivated you to that level of action and commitment?

GE: The detention of asylum seekers is unambiguously the worst thing that my own government is doing at present. Certainly indigenous Australians have been treated horrendously within my lifetime; they were effectively barred from voting until the 1960s, and they still suffer huge disadvantages in health and other social and economic matters. But the Aboriginal community itself is divided on exactly how the government ought to be responding to these problems, as are experts in the relevant policy fields, so for me personally this falls into the category of dire situations that I have no idea how to improve.

In contrast to that, every medically qualified person who's visited a detention center describes them with phrases like "factories for producing mental illness," and in any case it's just obvious to me that locking up people for years when they've committed no crime is barbaric. But I wasn't even aware that this was happening until the government started going to extremes to politicize the issue. In 2001 they sent armed commandoes to board a Norwegian freighter that had rescued asylum seekers from a boat that sank en route to Australia. The captain of the freighter wanted to allow the people he'd rescued to disembark on Australian territory—where they would have been taken straight into detention, so it wasn't even a matter of anyone entering the country undetected or unsupervised. But the government didn't want them entering Australia at all, so they used military force to prevent that, and then they bribed a small Pacific island, Nauru, to detain the asylum seekers there.

This was a hugely politically popular move, but my response was "You've got to be kidding." I never went to Nauru, but I finally found out what was happening in Australian detention centers, and that was every bit as appalling. And once I'd had some contact with the people who were actually locked up in those places, it was impossible to ignore what they were going through.

KB: There's some perennial debate about the extent to which science fiction can or should serve a predictive function. Do you ever write your stories specifically thinking about realistic predictions for the near future?

GE: It's never been my goal to predict the future. Of course, to create a believable backdrop for any story set in the future you have to give some thought to what's plausible on various time scales, and it can make the work more enjoyable if those details ring true and don't date too quickly. But I can forgive Philip K. Dick his weird mixture of carbon copies of typewritten documents and holidays on Jupiter so long as his central ideas are interesting in their own right, and I think in the end almost all science fiction will be judged the same way.

KB: Looking at your near-future SF over the years, have there been any cases that surprised you vis à vis how our future has unfolded?—in other words, something that you thought might be a long shot that seems to have proved out, or reasonable extrapolations that turned out to be off base?

GE: The speed with which digital communications technology became ubiquitous certainly makes some of my stories from the early 1990s look clunky. By the time I wrote *Distress* I think I got it pretty much right—everything in the world is searchable and available wirelessly, so Violet Mosala can pull a sound bite off the Web in seconds to correct a journalist at a press conference—but prior to that I was far too conservative. It's not that I didn't anticipate the potential of the technology, but I couldn't imagine that there'd be so much investment in actual infrastructure, and so quickly.

KB: Could you talk a little bit about your thought process with regard to developing the alien species and societies in *Incandescence* and the Orthogonal universe?

GE: As far as I can remember, those are the only two times I've written alien viewpoint characters, and in those books there were a lot of very specific constraints arising from other factors. So I can't really claim to have developed some overarching set of principles for writing about aliens.

But in those two cases, I've certainly adopted the approach of assuming that the aliens have sufficient mental agility such that their stream of consciousness can be meaningfully translated into ordinary narrative prose. It's plausible that most sophisticated evolved organisms would have analogs of things like hunger and satiety, pain and physical comfort, and drives related to whatever they do to reproduce, but to get any real story out of them they also need to be able to reflect on their own and other people's behaviour and to speculate on the consequences of different courses of action.

In *Incandescence* the aliens are the product of genetic engineering with a very particular set of goals, in that their ancestors have designed them to live stably for millions of years cooped up in a tiny ark, in the hope that some of these arks would survive when their home world was torn apart by a neutron star. By design, most of the population is completely satisfied with a life of repetitive agricultural work, with only a small fraction acting as a kind of sentinel for change, ready to respond if there's some unexpected shift in the environment that requires more flexibility.

For the Orthogonal books, I was thinking about various possibilities when it occurred to me that it would be interesting to have the protagonist's species reproduce by division. If a sentient organism divides, in principle that might work in either of two ways. There could be some retention of the parent's learned skills, and perhaps even some of their narrative memories—although with finite resources you couldn't go on endlessly accumulating memories down the generations. Or the division process could erase the parent's experience and leave the offspring starting afresh. I think either of these could be made plausible in a sufficiently alien biology, but in the end I chose the second mode. That led to a set of social and political issues that I think are interesting in their own right, and which seemed to complement the other main theme rather than obscuring it. Having a mind full of ancestral memories could make an interesting story—and I know people have done that, though I can't think of examples off the top of my head—but along with all the exotic physics in Orthogonal it would have made things overcomplicated.

KB: The Orthogonal universe stories delve into reproductive rights and gender politics in more depth than your previous work. Why did you choose to make that a central theme of that trilogy, along with the alternate universe physics?

GE: When I started planning Orthogonal, my main concern was simply to ensure that the biology of the aliens wasn't too similar to our own. But as soon as the idea of reproduction by division occurred to me, it was clear that it could work on all kinds of dramatic, emotional, and philosophical levels. All mothers die giving birth: how could that not be a source of enormous internal and external conflict?

We have a certain level of tension in our own species between people's conscious plans for their lives and the constraints our biology has imposed, but a premise like that amplifies the tension a thousandfold. And just as there's a range of responses to our own biology, I wanted these aliens to have attitudes spanning everything from complete acceptance to horror and revulsion. Obviously there would have to be strong enough drives and predispositions in this species to ensure that reproduction went ahead, but that doesn't imply some kind of blanket rule where their innate psychology would cause everyone to unequivocally embrace the whole thing.

Philosophically, this seemed like a perfect opportunity to explore the naturalistic fallacy: the idea that whatever nature has produced is the way things should be. In our own society this is sometimes bound up with religion, but I don't think that's the only way it arises. So although these aliens have no religion, many of them do take the attitude that nature provides a kind of ideal template for life, and their role is to accommodate to that, not to fight it.

As for the gender politics, if women are generally going to divide while they're still young enough for their co to raise the children, then in terms of political power they're starting out with a massive disadvantage. Apart from everything else, they'll literally be a minority, because of their much shorter life expectancy. I think it's almost inevitable that under these conditions most societies would start out with huge disparities in educational opportunity and reproductive choice.

I should stress, though, that none of this is meant to be read as an allegory for the human situation. My worst nightmare would be for some literal-minded gender studies academic to get hold of this book and start trying to map everything into mundane terms, with the division itself reduced to some kind of banal metaphor for societal attitudes to motherhood. My aim with the biology is very similar to my aim with the physics: to take the axioms seriously on their own terms, and allow the consequences to flow from that. Sometimes there are obvious parallels with our own society, just as there are similarities in the physics, but sometimes the results are utterly alien to us. Science fiction is wasted when it's used simply to crank out metaphors for familiar things; that's like mistaking a microscope for a paperweight.

KB: Also in *Incandescence* and Orthogonal, the researchers do everything they need to do without the benefit of electricity or computers. Was that a deliberate choice on your part, and if so, why?

GE: In *Incandescence*, the whole aim of the book was to watch science develop from a completely different starting point. I wanted a culture that couldn't observe bodies moving across the sky, the way we did for thousands of years, but nonetheless had a different set of clues accessible to them about the laws of motion and gravitational physics. Given the limitations on the size of the Splinter due to tidal forces, it wouldn't have made much sense for them to have developed any kind of well-resourced technological civilization while they were still cooped up inside this rock and still hadn't come to grips with the kind of science that described basic things like the weights of objects in different locations.

In the Orthogonal series something similar applies, but in that case the physics really forced the choice. The Riemannian space-time signature means there's no such thing as a massless particle, so photons must have rest mass. That causes electromagnetism to work very differently from our own version, in such a way that any kind of electronics would require far more advanced technology and a much deeper understanding of physics than we needed to reach the same level of utility. For example, their electrostatic and magnetostatic forces reverse direction on a microscopic scale, rather than maintaining the same direction the way they do in our universe, so you can't rub amber on cloth and pick up bits of paper, you can't play around with lodestones, you can't create a smooth voltage gradient with a battery that makes a current run through a conductor that makes a magnetic compass turn. So there's absolutely no prospect of mimicking the kind of discoveries and technology that came relatively easily to us throughout the nineteenth century. If Yalda's culture had had anything analogous to electronic computers, they could only have built them if they'd already answered all the questions and solved all the problems that the books are meant to be about.

KB: When it comes to questions of science and religion, Stephen Jay Gould advocated the "non-overlapping magisterial" view of things, where science and religion can coexist because they deal with separate domains of knowledge and inquiry. Your stories don't seem to share this view, often focusing on the worldviews in conflict. What is your take on the question of how science and religion coexist and conflict?

GE: Almost all religions make some range of factual claims about the world, and it's absurd to insulate those claims from rational scrutiny. If a religion asserts the existence of an immaterial soul or an afterlife, it makes perfect sense to examine these claims rationally, asking what the logical implications seem to be and how such things could coexist with what's actually known about our minds and bodies. Philosophers and theologians have spent centuries attempting to investigate all manner of religious claims in a rational manner—albeit with wildly varying degrees of honesty, competence, and intellectual freedom—but rather than bringing that practice to an end with some kind of truce, it ought to continue with much greater rigor.

Of course, there's a distinction between facts and values, and as David Hume argued, you can't derive an "ought" from an "is." But you can't derive an "ought" from a "God told me so" either. There will always be a potential for moral judgements to be disputed, and the way they're argued about and negotiated between people is a different process than the way factual scientific questions are settled. But that's no reason to surrender ground on moral issues to religious claims of revelation or authority.

KB: Do you ever worry that as time has gone on and your novels have focused more tightly on physics (particularly in *Incandescence* and the Orthogonal universe), that you're leaving some of your readers behind?

GE: There's an endless list of things an author can do that will annoy some readers of their previous books, but there's not a lot of point being a writer at all if you're going to let that dictate what you write about. For example, *Zendegi*, which is a very accessible book with no demanding technical content at all, had a hugely negative response from many readers who just weren't interested in the subjects I wanted to address in that novel.

Diaspora was more or less entirely about physics, and that's had the second best sales of any of my novels, after *Permutation City*. But what I've been aiming for with the physics in the later books is to make it much less hand-wavey and to write stories wherein the reader has to take as little as possible on faith. If I have any regret about *Incandescence*, it's that I failed to immerse the reader deeply enough in the intellectual revolution the Splinterites were going through. In the Orthogonal trilogy, the science is much simpler but also much broader, and you get to see the characters struggling with all the crucial details right before your eyes. One thing I'm really pleased about with *The Clockwork Rocket* is that the most important parts of it require no more background than Pythagoras's Theorem and similar triangles—ideas that are taught in primary school. In our own universe, a lot of supposedly arcane notions such as relativistic energy and momentum are really just primary-school geometry with a twist, and in the Orthogonal universe that twist has been removed so the ideas become even simpler.

Of course, the SF establishment is incredibly fusty and myopic when it comes to any significant use of science in science fiction. You can find critics who've spent their whole careers discussing the genre who don't think scientific discovery even counts as a form of narrative. But understanding how the universe works is by far the most important story in human history; nothing has had more impact on our lives. When Yalda deciphers the relationship between velocity and wavelength and realizes what it's telling her about the nature of light and the nature of time, that's the start of the most dramatic story in the history of her people.

KB: In 1993 you identified "Learning to Be Me" as your most successful story at the time in terms of your personal satisfaction with it. What is your answer to the same question today, in 2011?

GE: "Reasons to Be Cheerful." It's about the materiality of the person, which I think is one of the most important insights of the last three hundred years. But while a story like "Learning to Be Me" mines that same insight for a kind of eeriness and opacity, "Reasons to Be Cheerful" is more about demystifying it and coming to terms with it.

In some ways it's like an Oliver Sacks case study, where one of his patients experiences a terrible deficit as a result of some neurological injury, and of course those real-life case studies already drive home the fact that our personalities are physically grounded. But "Reasons to Be Cheerful" goes a step beyond that, by granting the protagonist a kind of restoration that gives him a deep understanding of the condition we're all in.

Also, I like the style and the protagonist's voice; I think they fit the subject matter as much as the plot does.

KB: In discussions of hard SF and characterization, your name comes up so often that people are starting to refer to the "Egan defense":

> . . . all of that can be forgiven because he brings to his work a unique interest in the character of physical law. Many science fiction writers pay homage to this subject, of course, but for most the laws of nature are there to serve the story: a discursion on the physics of a wormhole, say, would be for most writers an adjunct to a fantastic voyage therein, but Egan has the chutzpah to imagine that the reader will delight in the physics for its own sake. (Harrison)

Do you have any thoughts on that subject?

GE: I do find science intrinsically interesting, and I think it's perfectly legitimate to write fiction that's primarily concerned with scientific matters. There are readers who prefer science to be limited to various secondary roles in SF: a pure McGuffin to propel an adventure plot, a way of enabling some exotic technology, or a kind of backdrop to a sermon on the perils of ambition. All of these kinds of stories can be enjoyable, but I see no reason not to write fiction myself in which the science is absolutely central.

I don't doubt that there's a strand of literature where the main character is so entertaining that you wouldn't mind spending time with them regardless of the book's plot. But most fiction is interesting for other reasons, and the characters are there to collide with something outside themselves in order to reveal its shape—even if it's something as parochial as the cultural mores in an English village. In my own work, I suppose the relationship between the larger reality and the protagonist has fallen into two broad categories: sometimes it crashes over them like a wave they're trying to escape—that's what happens to Prabir in *Teranesia*, and Andrew in *Distress*—while in *Incandescence* and *The Clockwork Rocket*, the characters are actively pursuing the encounter long before it becomes a matter of urgency. The first mode comes from a tradition of protagonists simply trying to live their lives and being, as it were, mugged by Reality, whereas in the second mode the protagonists have seen Reality coming a mile off, made extensive notes about its movements, and started trying to figure out how it could be brought over to their side. And that second kind of plot can only work if the characters are curious about their world from the start.

Whether the particular characters are believable or appealing to particular readers is going to be a matter of their personal taste. Certainly Roi in *Incandescence* isn't a protagonist who's been chosen to evoke the feeling "Oh, I know someone just like that!" in anything other than her intellectual efforts, and that might be a problem for a reader with no personal experience of intellectual effort. Yalda in *The Clockwork Rocket* has a more complex set of relationships with friends and colleagues and family members, and though the alien biology that circumscribes her life is very different from our own, I don't think it's a huge stretch for any SF reader to empathize with her. She pushes against her culture's expectations on several levels, all the way from the farm where she's born to her treatment of a prisoner on a generation starship, but she's not any kind of saint, and she struggles when her adopted children get bratty. If there are readers for whom she remains unsatisfying, so be it, but that's no failure on my part, and there's nothing about her that needs to be "forgiven."

But to those who think it's the science that needs to be forgiven, what can I say? Most SF critics have only the sketchiest notion of what post-Enlightenment science has discovered, let alone twentieth-century physics, and they have no interest in investing any effort into engaging with the details. If I'd populated my novels with the kind of characters these people could relate to, Yalda would have spent all her time on the mountain trying to decide whether she was in love with Eusebio or Tullia, rotational physics would never have been discovered, no one would have thought of launching the Peerless, and the trilogy would have ended in one volume with an anticlimax rather like *Melancholia's*.

KB: Looking back on roughly twenty-five years in the field—achieving success, living as a full-time writer, becoming one of the key figures of SF (particularly hard SF)—how do you feel about what you've accomplished so far? What are your hopes for your writing in the future?

GE: If I think back on all the individual works that I've published, I have a range of reactions: there are things I'm still very pleased with, and others that look pretty clunky in retrospect. But overall I'm glad that I've ended up spending my time this way.

If I'm pleased with one general achievement, it's to have contributed something to the very small subset of literature that engages in a meaningful way with the full context of human existence. The fact that we are part of a physical universe whose laws can be discovered through reason and observation is the most profound and powerful insight in our history, but most literature—including a large proportion of SF—either ignores it or trivializes it. I'm not interested in fiction that invites the reader to become slack-jawed with "wonder" at the size of the universe or the time scale of cosmology or the strangeness of quantum mechanics, or that treats the now-long-obvious fact that there is no God and we have no preexisting purpose as some kind of belittling revelation of our insignificance and impermanence. Literature that truly engages with reality isn't shocked by things we've known for centuries; rather, it delights in the fact that we've managed to learn so much about the universe, and it revels in the details.

A body of art that contained nothing about the laws of electromagnetism, gravity, and quantum mechanics, nothing about the physical grounding of consciousness, and nothing about the process by which we've learnt the rules that govern everything around us, would be like a body of art depicting present day Earth that contained no mention of any human law or custom, no tension between an individual and society, and no representation of a city, a village, a forest or a river. Art that's blind to the true landscape we inhabit—physical reality in the widest sense—is just absurdly, pathetically blinkered and myopic.

So while I'm sure that the individual works I've written have only succeeded to varying degrees, I'm still proud to have done something to nudge the center of gravity of contemporary SF some microscopic distance toward a genuine engagement with reality.

What I hope for in the future is to keep doing that, more energetically than ever.

A Greg Egan Bibliography

Greg Egan has published twelve novels and sixty short stories so far. For this bibliography I have chosen to list all of his novels in chronological order as well as a selection of his significant short fiction. In all cases the bibliographic information comes from the original publication listed on Egan's professional website and has been corroborated using the Internet Speculative Fiction Database. All of Egan's books except *An Unusual Angle* are currently available as e-books, usually through the U.S., U.K., or Australian Amazon Kindle stores.

An Unusual Angle, 1983 (Norstrilia Press). No current in-print edition.
"The Cutie." *Interzone* 29, May/June 1989.
"Eugene." *Interzone* 36, June 1990.
"Learning to Be Me." *Interzone* 37, July 1990.
"The Safe-Deposit Box." *Isaac Asimov's Science Fiction Magazine*, September 1990.
"Axiomatic." *Interzone* 41, November 1990.
"Blood Sisters." *Interzone* 44, February 1991.
"Closer." *Eidolon* 9, Winter 1992.
Quarantine, 1992 (Century/Legend). Out of print.
"The Hundred Light-Year Diary." *Interzone* 55, January 1992.
"Unstable Orbits in the Space of Lies." *Interzone* 61, July 1992.
"Cocoon." *Asimov's Science Fiction*, May 1994.
Permutation City, 1994 (Orion/Millennium).
"A Kidnapping." *Axiomatic*, 1995 (Orion/Millennium).
Distress, 1995 (Orion/Millennium).
"Mitochondrial Eve." *Interzone* 92, February 1995.
"Luminous." *Asimov's Science Fiction*, September 1995.
"Mister Volition." *Interzone* 100, October 1995.
"TAP." *Asimov's Science Fiction*, November 1995.
"Silver Fire." *Interzone* 102, December 1995.
"Wang's Carpets." *New Legends*, ed. Greg Bear, 1995 (Legend).
Diaspora, 1997 (Orion/Millennium).
"Reasons to Be Cheerful." *Interzone* 118. April 1997.
"The Planck Dive." *Asimov's Science Fiction*, February 1998.

"Oceanic." *Asimov's Science Fiction*, August 1998.
Teranesia, 1999 (Orion/Gollancz).
"Oracle." *Asimov's Science Fiction*, July 2000.
Schild's Ladder, 2002 (Orion/Gollancz).
"Singleton." *Interzone* 176, February 2002.
"Dark Integers." *Asimov's Science Fiction*, October/November 2007.
"Glory." *The New Space Opera*, ed. Gardner Dozois and Jonathan Strahan, 2007 (Eos).
"Crystal Nights." *Interzone* 215, April 2008.
Incandescence, 2008 (Orion/Gollancz).
Zendegi, 2010 (Orion/Gollancz).
Orthogonal Book One: The Clockwork Rocket, 2011 (Night Shade).
Orthogonal Book Two: The Eternal Flame, 2012 (Night Shade).
Orthogonal Book Three: The Arrows of Time, 2013 (Orion/Gollancz).

WORKS CITED

Blackford, Russell, ed. "Symposium on Posthuman Science Fiction. Gregory Benford, Maureen Kincaid Speller, Andrew M. Butler, Helen Merrick, Joe Haldeman." *Foundation* 78 (2000): 83–103.

———. "Transhumanism Still at the Crossroads." *Metamagician and the Hellfire Club,* April 22, 2008. Available at http://metamagician3000.blogspot.co.uk/2008_04_01_archive.html (accessed November 17, 2012).

Bordo, Susan. *Unbearable Weight: Feminism, Western Culture, and the Body*. 10th Anniversary Edition. Los Angeles: University of California Press. 1993, 2003.

Bould, Mark, Andrew M. Butler, Adam Roberts, Sherryl Vint. *Fifty Key Figures in Science Fiction*. New York: Routledge, 2010.

Bowling, Jill, and Martin, Brian. "Science: A Masculine Disorder?" *Science and Public Policy* 12 (1985): 6.

Burnham, Karen. "Inconstant Constants." *Clarkesworld* 59 (2011). Available at http://clarkesworldmagazine.com/burnham_08_11/ (accessed November 17, 2012).

Clute, John. "Unhampered." *Interzone* 86 (1994).

Dick, Philip K. "How to Build a Universe That Doesn't Fall Apart Two Days Later." 1978. Available at http://deoxy.org/pkd_how2build.htm (accessed November 17, 2012).

Egan, Greg. "Anatomy of a Hatchet Job." Available at http://www.gregegan.net/INCANDESCENCE/Z/Hatchet.html (accessed November 17, 2012).

———. *Aurealis* Interview, by Russell Blackford. *Aurealis* 42 (2009). Available at http://www.gregegan.net/INTERVIEWS/Interviews.html#Aurealis (accessed November 17, 2012).

———. *Axiomatic*. London: Gollancz, 2008.

———. "The Big Idea: Greg Egan." *Whatever*, July 22, 2008. Available at http://whatever.scalzi.com/2008/07/22/the-big-idea-greg-egan/ (accessed November 17, 2012).

———. "Booked! Greg Egan, Author, *The Clockwork Rocket*." *Suvudu*, September 25, 2011. Available at http://suvudu.com/2011/09/booked-greg-egan-author-the-clockwork-rocket.html (accessed November17, 2012).

———. "Born Again, Briefly." Available at http://www.gregegan.net/ESSAYS/BAB/BAB.html (accessed November 17, 2012).

———. "Burning the Motherhood Statements: An Interview with Greg Egan." *Eidolon: The Journal of Australian Science Fiction and Fantasy* 11 (1993). Available at http://eidolon.net/eidolon_magazine/issue_11/11_egan.htm (accessed November 17, 2012).

———. *The Clockwork Rocket*. San Francisco: Night Shade, 2011.
———. *Crystal Nights and Other Stories*. Burton, Mich.: Subterranean, 2009.
———. *Dark Integers and Other Stories*. Burton, Mich.: Subterranean, 2008.
———. *Diaspora*. New York: HarperPrism, 1998.
———. *Distress*. New York: HarperPrism, 1998.
———. *The Eternal Flame*. San Francisco: Night Shade, 2012. E-book.
———. *Incandescence*. San Francisco: Night Shade, 2008.
———. "Interview: Virtual Worlds and Imagined Freedoms." *Albedo One* (2009). Available at http://www.albedo1.com/?page_id=303 (accessed November 17, 2012).
———. *Luminous*. London: Gollancz, 2008.
———. *noise!* interview, by Marisa O'Keeffe. *noise!* (1998). Available at http://www.gregegan.net/INTERVIEWS/Interviews.html#noise (accessed November 17, 2012).
———. "*Permutation City*: The Dust Theory FAQ." Available at http://wwwgregegan.net/PERMUTATION/FAQ/FAQ.html (accessed November 17, 2012).
———. "Plus, Minus: A Gentle Introduction to the Physics of *Orthogonal*." Available at http://gregegan.net/ORTHOGONAL/00/PM.html (accessed November 17, 2012).
———. "Quantum Mechanics and Quarantine." Available at http://www.gregegan.net/QUARANTINE/QM/QM.html (accessed November 17, 2012).
———. "A Report on the Origins and Hazardous Effects of Miracle Ingredient A." *Eidolon: The Journal of Australian Science Fiction and Fantasy* 17/18, 1995. Available at http://eidolon.net/eidolon_magazine/issue_17/17_egan.htm (accessed November 17, 2012).
———. *Schild's Ladder*. New York: EOS, 2002.
———. "Steve Fever." *Technology Review* (Nov/Dec 2007).
———. *Teranesia*. New York: EOS, 2000.
———. *An Unusual Angle*. Carlton, Victoria: Norstrilia, 1983.
———. "Yeyuka." Infinity Plus. Available at http://www.infinityplus.co.uk/stories/yeyuka.htm (accessed November 17, 2012).
———. *Zendegi*. San Francisco: Night Shade Books, 2011.
"Egan, Greg." *The Encyclopedia of Science Fiction*, 3rd ed. Available at http://sf-encyclopedia.com/entry/egan_greg (accessed September 29, 2012).
Eidolon: The Journal of Australian Science Fiction and Fantasy. (1990–2000).
Gibson, William. "The Science in Science Fiction" *NPR's Talk of the Nation*. November 30, 1999. Radio Broadcast.
Gleick, James. *The Information: A History, A Theory, A Flood*. New York: Pantheon, 2011.
Hartwell, David, and Kathryn Cramer. *The Ascent of Wonder: The Evolution of Hard SF.* New York, Tor, 1994.
———. *The Hard SF Renaissance*. New York: Orb, 2002.
Hayles, N. Katherine. *How We Became Post Human: Virtual Bodies in Cybernetics, Literature, and Informatics*. Chicago: University of Chicago Press, 1999.
———. *My Mother Was a Computer: Digital Subjects and Literary Texts*. Chicago: University of Chicago Press, 2005. E-book.
Hodges, Andrew. *Alan Turing: The Enigma*. New York: Walker, 2000.
James, Edward, and Mendlesohn, Farah. *The Cambridge Companion to Science Fiction*. Cambridge: Cambridge University Press, 2003.
Jones, Gwyneth. "*Diaspora* by Greg Egan." *Foundation* 72 (1998).

Kurzweil, Ray. *The Singularity is Near: When Humans Transcend Biology*, New York: Viking, 2005.
Letson, Russell. "*Permutation City* by Greg Egan." *Locus* 405 (1994).
Locus Roundtable on Greg Egan. March 4, 2012. Available at http://www.locusmag.com/Roundtable/2012/03/roundtable-on-greg-egan/ (accessed November 17, 2012).
Locus Roundtable: Karen Burnham and Ted Chiang in Conversation. April 21, 2012. Available at http://www.locusmag.com/Roundtable/2011/04/karen-burnham-and-ted-chiang-in-conversation (accessed November 17, 2012). Podcast.
Mann, George. *The Mammoth Encyclopedia of Science Fiction*. New York: Carroll & Graf, 2001.
Maslow, Abraham H. *The Psychology of Science: A Reconnaissance*. Chicago: Regnery, 1966.
Mason, T.J. "Letter." *Interzone* 40 (1990).
McCalmont, Jonathan M. "*Incandescence* by Greg Egan." *SF Site* 2008. Available at http://www.sfsite.com/09a/ic279.htm (accessed November 17, 2012).
McKibben, Bill. *Enough: Staying Human in an Engineered Age*. New York: Owl/ Holt, 2003.
Midgley, Mary. *Science as Salvation: A Modern Myth and its Meaning*. New York: Routledge, 1992.
Minsky, Marvin. *The Society of Mind*. New York: Touchstone/Simon & Schuster, 1998.
Moravec, Hans. *Mind Children: The Future of Robot and Human Intelligence*. Cambridge: Harvard University Press, 1988.
Orzel, Chad. *How to Teach Physics to Your Dog*. New York: Scribner, 2009. E-book.
———. *How to Teach Relativity to Your Dog*. New York: Basic, 2012. E-book.
Passmore, John. *Science and Its Critics*. New Brunswick, N.J.: Rutgers University Press, 1978.
Roberts, Adam. "*Incandescence* by Greg Egan." June 6, 2008. Available at http://www.strangehorizons.com/reviews/2008/06/incandescence_b.shtml (accessed November 17, 2012).
———. "Greg Egan: The Clockwork Rocket (2011)." *Punkadiddle* 9 (March 2012). Available at http://punkadiddle.blogspot.com/2012/03/greg-egan-clockwork-rocket-orthogonal.html (accessed November 17, 2012).
Sandberg, Anders. "*Diaspora* by Greg Egan." October 17, 1997. Available at http://extropians.weidai.com/extropians.4Q97/0598.html (accessed November 17, 2012).
SF Signal (blog). "Mind Meld: Is SF Still the 'Big Idea' Genre?" May 23, 2012. Available at http://www.sfsignal.com/archives/2012/05/mind-meld-is-sf-still-the-big-idea-genre/ (accessed November 17, 2012).
Stableford, Brian. "*Quarantine* by Greg Egan." *New York Review of Science Fiction* 53 (1993).
Strange Horizons (blog). "Reading Egan." December 29, 2011. Available at http://www.strangehorizons.com/blog/2011/12/gareth_rees_takes_on_that.shtml#c592342 (accessed November 17, 2012).
Walton, Jo. "To Trace Impunity: Greg Egan's *Permutation City*." *Tor.com*. September 16, 2008. Available at http://www.tor.com/blogs/2008/09/egan (accessed November 17, 2012).
Wolfe, Gary K. "*Permutation City* by Greg Egan." *Locus* 401 (June 1994).

INDEX

KAREN BURNHAM works as a physicist and engineer at NASA's Johnson Space Center.

Modern Masters of Science Fiction

John Brunner *Jad Smith*

William Gibson *Gary Westfahl*

Gregory Benford *George Slusser*

Greg Egan *Karen Burnham*

THE UNIVERSITY OF ILLINOIS PRESS
is a founding member of the
Association of American University Presses.

Designed by Kelly Gray
Composed in 10.75/14.5 Dante
with Univers display
by Celia Shapland
at the University of Illinois Press
Manufactured by Sheridan Books, Inc.

University of Illinois Press
1325 South Oak Street
Champaign, IL 61820-6903
www.press.uillinois.edu